A

THE END

ENCOUNTERING THE SUBVERSIVE

OF

SPIRITUALITY OF JESUS

~~RELIGION~~

BRUXY CAVEY

HERALD
P R E S S

Harrisonburg, Virginia

Herald Press
PO Box 866, Harrisonburg, Virginia 22803
www.HeraldPress.com

Designed to be used with *The End of Religion: Encountering the Subversive Spirituality of Jesus*, expanded edition, 978-1-5138-0549-8, $18.99 USD.

THE END OF RELIGION: A STUDY COMPANION
© 2021 by Bruxy Cavey
Released by Herald Press, Harrisonburg, Virginia 22803. 800-245-7894.
    All rights reserved.
Library of Congress Control Number: 2021940364
International Standard Book Number: 978-1-5138-0866-6 (paperback); 978-1-5138-0867-3 (ebook)
Printed in United States of America

25 24 23 22 21   10 9 8 7 6 5 4 3 2 1

CONTENTS

Introduction: Are You Ready to Rethink? 5

SESSION 1: Go and Learn 11
Preface, Introduction, and Chapters 1 and 2

SESSION 2: Grace and Peace 15
Chapters 3, 4, 5, and 6

SESSION 3: The End and the Beginning 19
Chapters 7 and 8

SESSION 4: Torah and Tradition 23
Chapters 9 and 10

SESSION 5: Tribalism and Territory 27
Chapters 11 and 12

SESSION 6: Temple, Symbols, and Sacrifice 33
Chapters 13, 14, and 15

SESSION 7: Resurrection and Ascension 39
Chapters 16 and 17

SESSION 8: Who Was (and Is) Jesus? 43
Chapters 18, 19, and 20

SESSION 9: The Way of Love 47
Chapters 21, 22, 23, and 24

SESSION 10: The Irreligious Life 51
Chapters 25, 26, 27, and Epilogue

Bonus Chapter 1: The Faith Instinct 55

Bonus Chapter 2: The Origin of Religion 71

Appendix A: Toward a Jesus-Centered Spiritual Practice 85

Appendix B: Continuing Education 99

Notes 103

The Author 111

Introduction

ARE YOU READY TO RETHINK?

Jesus came to change our minds, our hearts, and our lives. His invitation to all of us into this experience of change can be summed up in his two-word encouragement to "repent and believe" (Mark 1:15).

REPENT AND BELIEVE

For some of us, when we read those words on this page—repent and believe—our default mental image might be a Bible-thumping preacher shouting at us in an accusatory tone with lots of finger-pointing: *Ree-pennnt!!*

The truth is, to repent simply means to change our minds about something: literally, to re-think. It's really a beautiful word. We often think of repentance in terms of feeling remorseful about our sins. Jesus uses the word *repent* this way sometimes (e.g., Luke 17:3-4). But more often, Jesus calls us to repent (rethink our lives), not in terms of the bad we have done, but in terms of the good *Jesus is doing* (e.g., Matthew 4:17). When we repent, we rethink, and as a result we recommit to a new focus for our lives and a new course of action. Repentance is a matter not just of feeling bad about our *past*, but of becoming hope-filled about our *future*. When we encounter Christ, he brings about new things in our lives, and our job is simply to be ready to repent, ready to rethink everything.

And then there is that second word: *believe*. When Jesus invites us to believe, or to have faith, or to trust (all the same word in the biblical languages), he most often invites us not just to believe *that* something is true, but to trust *in* a person: him (e.g., John 6:35; 7:38-39; 11:25; 12:44-46; 14:1; 17:21). To believe *in* someone, rather than merely believe *what* a person says or *that* a thing is true, means that faith should be deeply *personal* ("I trust you") and not just *propositional* ("I believe that"). It means to consider someone as trustworthy and to make ourselves trustworthy to them, to perceive someone as faithful and so to become faithful toward them. In the Bible, the word *faith* refers to a dynamic that connects persons together in a faithful relationship.

Over the course of this ten-part study, I am inviting us all to "repent and believe"—to be open to changing our minds about what we thought we knew and to be willing to trust in the person, the message, and the way of Jesus moving forward. This *trust in* Jesus includes making ourselves *trustworthy to* Jesus. Having *faith in* Jesus means becoming *faithful to* Jesus. We are talking about changing our minds, yes, but what use is changing our minds for the better if it doesn't change how we live and who we become? So I am inviting us all to consider committing to Christ, pledging our allegiance to Jesus, making Jesus our main operating principle, our spiritual center, and our guiding orientation.

Of course, you may not want to accept this offer. You may not become convinced, as I am, that Jesus is everything he claimed to be and that we would all be better off if we made our pledge of allegiance to Jesus. Even so, this study will still be time well spent for you. You will, at the very least, learn more about the single most influential human life in history.

In the words of this early twentieth-century poem about the historical Jesus:

All the armies that ever marched,
all the navies that were ever built,
all the parliaments that ever sat and
all the kings that ever reigned,
put together,
have not affected
the life of man upon this earth
as powerfully as has this one solitary life.[1]

By the name of Jesus, billions of people curse. And in the name of Jesus, billions of people pray. And by taking time to learn more about Jesus, we are learning more about ourselves.[2]

THE NEW COVENANT

If you open up a Christian Bible, you will notice that it is divided into two parts: the Old Testament and the New Testament. The Old Testament records the time before Jesus, when Israel lived according to the Old Covenant (*covenant* and *testament* mean the same thing: a way of being in relationship). The New Testament records the life and teachings of Jesus and the writings and struggles of his first generation of followers as they lived out this New Covenant way of being in relationship with God and one another.

In essence, the Old Covenant was the way of law, and the New Covenant is the way of love. The apostle John describes the New Covenant as the way of truth and grace replacing the way of law (John 1:17), and the apostle Paul describes it as the new way of the Spirit replacing the old way of just following the words on the page (2 Corinthians 3:6).

This seismic shift in religious history was prophesied in the Jewish scriptures (what Christian Bibles identify as the "Old Testament"), making them the most courageous and hope-filled religious texts imaginable. Think of it: the Jewish faith has embedded within it the promise of the Messiah coming to bring an end to his own religion under its current structure. This would be like the Pope declaring the end of Catholicism or the Dalai Lama declaring the end of Tibetan Buddhism.

Jesus of Nazareth claimed that he was the long-awaited Messiah of the Jewish people, and that as their Messiah he had come to transition humankind into a new way of being in relationship with God and one another, called the New Covenant. His teachings would prepare people for this New Covenant life. His own life would model what he taught. And his death would actualize the New Covenant in blood.

The result would be a kind of resurrection, literally and figuratively. Jesus would rise again to show us all the way forward: a way of radical forgiveness (even toward enemies), a way of amazing grace replacing fastidious moralism, a way of unconditional love replacing religious rule-keeping, and a way of Spirit-infused intimacy and empowerment replacing the human struggle to satisfactorily obey religious teachers and texts.

Jesus. Changes. Everything.

And this is why I am excited for all of us on this journey together. No matter who you are or what you believe, the fact that you are investing time and attention in Jesus is the most exciting thing you could be doing right now.

THE SPIRITUAL SPECTRUM

Some of us in this study are new to the whole Jesus thing, with loads to learn. And some of us are seasoned veterans, with loads to *un*learn. Either way, we have all arrived at the same place at the same time: ready to receive something from the study of Jesus.

If you are new to understanding Christian spirituality, consider yourself fortunate. Jesus found that his message was most resisted and most rejected by people who felt they had life and scripture and God already all figured out. So longtime religious Christians may have lots to *deconstruct* before they can *reconstruct* a healthy relationship with God through Jesus. Changing our minds, especially about something in which we have invested years of energy, is hard. Nonbelievers or people on the religious margins might have less they need to say *no* to in order to say *yes* to the way of Jesus.

Wherever you find yourself on the continuum of religion and spirituality, we can all help each other with our spiritual growth through the observations we bring, the questions we ask, and the encouragement we give.

GETTING THE MOST OUT OF THIS STUDY

Each session is designed to last for one to two hours. They are divided into four sections:

a. *Highlights* is your link to a "highlight reel" video that will review some key points and introduce some new thoughts. You can decide as a group if you are going to watch this together as part of your session or separately before each session.

b. *Hang Out* is your chance to talk about what stood out to you from the relevant chapters of *The End of Religion*, with some optional questions if your discussion needs some help. Use these questions like a menu, not a checklist. In other words, these questions are options to choose from rather than a to-do list you need to complete. (Questions that are ones not to miss or skip are marked with a ★.)

c. *Hear* is your time to open up that other book—the Bible—and learn even more, straight from the source documents. The relevant texts are printed in the study guide, but if you have your own Bible, feel free to bring it to the sessions so you can read the context and mark it up. (I find that under-lining verses that speak to me, circling key words, and making notes in the margins enhances my Bible study.)

d. *Huddle* is an opportunity to pause and make it personal, to listen to what God might be saying to you, to share with your group, and to pray, if you are open to that.

Pro tip 1: If your book study group is large, try breaking into subgroups: keep your Hang Out and Hear groups under a dozen, and your Huddles to under a half dozen.

Pro tip 2: Please come to each session having read the suggested chapters and ready to talk about whatever stood out to you.

Pro tip 3: If you have any lingering questions, feel free to get in touch with me. With a name like Bruxy Cavey, I am pretty easy to find on social media.

SPOILER ALERT

Before we begin the first session, I need to tell you about the end of *The End of Religion*. As you progress through the latter few chapters of the book, it will become increasingly clear that Jesus came not only to *end* religion, but to *begin* something beautiful: a spiritual family rooted in love. Jesus came not only to help people (re)connect with God, but to help people (re)connect with one another. Jesus did not promote an individualistic, purely vertical, just-me-and-God spirituality. Instead, Jesus encourages his followers to worship God horizontally, by loving one another well.

So it would be a bit of a miss if we did a book study about the subversive spirituality of Jesus and didn't lean in and learn from one another, opening our hearts for God to speak *to* us *through* one another, and *through* us *to* one another.

With this in mind, I'm encouraging all of us to pay attention, not only to the content of the book but also to the lives of the people with whom we are discussing it. (If you are going through this study guide alone, I'm so glad you are investing the time. My only recommendation is that you find some way to discuss what you are learning with at least one other person to make this a relational experience.) Those of us who are more comfortable talking may need to leave space to tease out the thoughts of those who are quieter. And those of us who are more reserved may need to find the courage to communicate our own thoughts and questions more often.

Here is our chance to do more than learn new ideas. Here is our chance to begin to form new friendships and forge new family. At least, this can be a first step. And if you are listening closely, in every session you may hear the voice of the Spirit of Christ inviting you to repent and believe.

Session 1

GO AND LEARN

Preface, Introduction, Chapters 1 and 2

HIGHLIGHTS

www.bruxy.com/theendofreligionstudy1

HANG OUT

1. ★ The introduction of this study invites you to be prepared to rethink and trust (repent and believe) in the person, teaching, and way of Jesus. Starting out, on a scale of 1–10, how ready do you think you are to experience a spiritual shift in your life?

   a. I'm so ready I could burst! (8–10 out of 10)
   b. I'm eager but cautious. (6–7 out of 10)
   c. I'm neutral. (5 out of 10)
   d. I'm mostly skeptical, but open. (3–4 out of 10)
   e. I'm doing it, but I ain't diggin' it. (1–2 out of 10)
   f. It's complicated. Let me explain . . .

2. ★ From this session's assigned reading, what stood out to you? Share interesting highlights or lingering questions. (Note: This same question will begin the "Hang Out" section of each session, and if it is all you get to, then that is enough.)

3. What is the value of basing our investigation and understanding of Jesus on the Bible, rather than on other ancient post-biblical literature?

4. A close read of John 2 reveals that the water turns into wine only when the servants actually follow Jesus' instructions to serve it to others. Jesus does not perform the miracle by himself first and then allow the servants to tell others about it. Rather, their faith, their participation, and their courage to obey become part of the transformation. What lessons are in this for us?

5. ★ Many religious leaders of Jesus' day (and throughout church history) missed the point of his teaching because of their preconceived notions and institutional biases.

   a. As we start this journey, what do you think are some of *your* unseen biases or hidden agendas when approaching the topics of God, Jesus, the Bible, and faith?

   b. How might these biases potentially clarify or cloud your view of truth?

HEAR

As Jesus went on from there, he saw a man named Matthew sitting at the tax collector's booth. "Follow me," he told him, and Matthew got up and followed him.

While Jesus was having dinner at Matthew's house, many tax collectors and sinners came and ate with him and his disciples. When the Pharisees saw this, they asked his disciples, "Why does your teacher eat with tax collectors and sinners?"

On hearing this, Jesus said, "It is not the healthy who need a doctor, but the sick. But go and learn what this means: 'I desire mercy, not sacrifice.' For I have not come to call the righteous, but sinners."

—MATTHEW 9:9-13

6. ★ Read Matthew 9:9-13.

   a. ★ What stands out to you from this passage?

b. What do you think is the importance of Jesus saying "follow *me*" rather than "follow God" or "follow the Spirit" or "follow the Bible" or "follow love" or "follow truth" or something else?

c. What do you think about Jesus dividing people into "healthy/righteous" on one side and "sick/sinners" on the other? Do you think Jesus really thinks the religious leaders he is talking to are spiritually "healthy"? Talk about Jesus' use of irony. (Also see Luke 18:9-14 for more on Jesus' view of who is really "healthy" and who is really "sick.")

d. ★ Over these ten sessions we are trying to live out this one instruction from Jesus, to "go and learn what this means: 'I desire mercy, not sacrifice.'" If you were a character in this story, who would you be?

    i. A religious leader assessing what's going on

    ii. A disciple of Jesus committed to learning

    iii. A sinner surprised by the inclusivity of Christ

    iv. Sir Not-Appearing-in-This-Film (sorry, another Monty Python reference)

HUDDLE

7. ★ Name one new thing you are learning . . .

a. about God

b. about yourself

8. Prayer option: If time permits and you feel comfortable doing so, take time to pray for one another, that you might hear God's voice this week—through *The End of Religion*, the Bible, prayer, meditation, art, nature, an internal witness, and/or conversations with the people in your lives. Invite God's Spirit to speak, and commit to keeping your spiritual ears open. (Note: If you're comfortable with it, exchange contact information and touch base between sessions to see how you're doing and what you're learning.)

Session 2

GRACE AND PEACE

Chapters 3, 4, 5, and 6

HIGHLIGHTS

www.bruxy.com/theendofreligionstudy2

HANG OUT

1. ★ From this session's assigned reading, what stood out to you? Share interesting highlights or lingering questions.
2. Have you tended to use the words *religion* and *religious* positively or negatively?

    a. What are some synonyms for the positive use of the word *religion*?
    b. What are some synonyms for the negative use of the word *religion*?

3. How can religion function like Stockholm syndrome?
4. How can the doctrines of karma and reincarnation lead to increased human suffering?
5. Why is it sub-Christian (and even dangerous) for Christians to "follow the Bible" (as opposed to following Jesus)?

HEAR

> For the wages of sin is death, but the gift of God is eternal life in Christ Jesus our Lord.
>
> **—ROMANS 6:23**

> For it is by grace you have been saved, through faith—and this is not from yourselves, it is the gift of God—not by works, so that no one can boast. For we are God's handiwork, created in Christ Jesus to do good works, which God prepared in advance for us to do.
>
> **—EPHESIANS 2:8-10**

6. ★ Read Romans 6:23 and Ephesians 2:8-10 (and the entire chapter of Luke 15, if time permits).

   a. ★ What stands out to you from these passages?

   b. ★ All of these passages describe the amazingness of grace in different ways: receiving a gift instead of paying a wage; salvation leading to good works rather than the other way around; and being surprised by your Father's joyful forgiveness and lavish love, even when you've messed up big time. Why is grace so threatening to the way of religion?

   c. If you've read Luke 15, do you tend to be more like the little brother or the older brother in Jesus' parable of the prodigal son?

   d. If time permits, take five to ten minutes for quiet meditation, silently reading over these passages again while you locate yourself in their teaching, and let your heart be graced by God.

7. Side project: The topic of the peace teachings of Jesus will come up again later in the book, but for now, I want to plant a seed in our minds as we process the issue of violence and church history on our own time. Read Matthew 5:38-47;

Luke 6:27-36; Romans 12:17-21; and 1 John 3:16; also, keep in mind the way Jesus lived, and died, and lived again.

a. What stands out to you from these passages?

b. History lesson time! The Christian church has been divided into two positions on the peace teachings of Jesus and how we should apply them to the issue of violence. For the first three hundred years of church history, the majority position was nonviolent activism (called *pacifism*)—the belief that Christ-followers are called to be nonviolent, enemy-loving peacemakers. But as the church gained more political influence, the majority view shifted from pacifism to just war theory, which teaches that under certain circumstances, violence by Christians is allowable.

"Just war" Christians believe that military service and policing, as well as certain private situations (e.g., responding to home invasions with potentially lethal violence), are exceptions to the way of nonviolent enemy love that Jesus teaches in his Sermon on the Mount. Some just war Christians teach that Jesus encouraged his pacifist perspective only for his immediate twelve disciples, or perhaps for a special elite class of committed monks and nuns throughout the centuries, but not for all Christ-followers of all times in all contexts. All just war proponents advocate that Christians need to balance the teaching of Jesus with the examples of Moses, Joshua, David, and the prophets of the Old Testament, who sometimes encouraged violence for righteous reasons (e.g., see Psalm 149:6-9). This has been the dominant Christian view since the fourth century, although ever since the Radical Reformation in the sixteenth century, a growing movement of Christians have promoted a return to the nonviolent, enemy-loving peace teachings of Jesus. So what do *you* think?

HUDDLE

8. ★ Name one new thing you are learning . . .
   a. about God
   b. about yourself

9. Self-assessment: Can you think of ways you tend to use faith and spirituality as mirrors instead of windows?

10. Prayer option: If time permits and you feel comfortable doing so, take time to pray for one another, that you might hear God's voice this week—through *The End of Religion*, the Bible, prayer, meditation, art, nature, an internal witness, and/or conversations with each other. Invite God's Spirit to speak, and commit to keeping your spiritual ears open. (Again note: If you're comfortable with it, exchange contact information and touch base between sessions to see how you're doing and what you're learning.)

Session 3

THE END AND THE BEGINNING

Chapters 7 and 8

HIGHLIGHTS

www.bruxy.com/theendofreligionstudy3

HANG OUT

1. ★ From this session's assigned reading, what stood out to you? Share interesting highlights or lingering questions.
2. How is religion like spiritual hoarding? Can you think of any examples from your own religious life, or from church history?
3. In your own words, how is Jesus the "end" of religion?
4. Why is it important to study the teachings of Jesus within their first-century Jewish context? How can this help us draw out the universal truths for our lives today?
5. No religion or philosophy or spiritual practice offers what the New Covenant brings. The entire idea expressed through the New Covenant is completely unique. Reread the section called "Extreme Makeover" on pages 103–4 of *The End of Religion*. In fancy theological words, this section describes moving beyond the idea of *imputation* (being *declared* or *considered* righteous by God) to *impartation* (actually being *made* or *re-created* righteous by God). The Protestant

Reformation (began c. 1517) was focused on and fueled by the idea of imputation: justification by faith alone. One Protestant Reformer, Martin Luther, is rumored to have said that justification (imputed righteousness) makes Christians like "snow-covered dung": the same on the inside, but covered with the righteousness of Christ on the outside. On the other hand, the Radical Reformation (began c. 1525) emphasized the idea of impartation (being truly reborn, regenerated, and renewed from the inside out). This imparted righteousness actually and truly makes us into new-and-improved versions of ourselves!

Talk about how this New Covenant understanding of our identity (actual imparted righteousness) can affect our sense of self, and our way of engaging with others.

6. During long seasons of church history, Christians interpreted Jesus' condemnation of many Jewish *practices* as God's condemnation of Jewish *people*. This misrepresentation of Jesus fueled Christian antisemitism for centuries. What steps can we take to avoid making this destructive mistake today?

HEAR

"The days are coming," declares the Lord,
    "when I will make a new covenant
with the people of Israel
    and with the people of Judah.
It will not be like the covenant
    I made with their ancestors
when I took them by the hand
    to lead them out of Egypt,
because they broke my covenant,
    though I was a husband to them,"
        declares the Lord.
"This is the covenant I will make with the people of Israel
    after that time," declares the Lord.
"I will put my law in their minds
    and write it on their hearts.

I will be their God,
  and they will be my people.
No longer will they teach their neighbor,
  or say to one another, 'Know the LORD,'
because they will all know me,
  from the least of them to the greatest,"
    declares the LORD.
"For I will forgive their wickedness
  and will remember their sins no more."

—**JEREMIAH 31:31-34**

I will give them an undivided heart and put a new spirit in them; I will remove from them their heart of stone and give them a heart of flesh. Then they will follow my decrees and be careful to keep my laws. They will be my people, and I will be their God.

—**EZEKIEL 11:19-20**

I will sprinkle clean water on you, and you will be clean; I will cleanse you from all your impurities and from all your idols. I will give you a new heart and put a new spirit in you; I will remove from you your heart of stone and give you a heart of flesh. And I will put my Spirit in you and move you to follow my decrees and be careful to keep my laws.

—**EZEKIEL 36:25-27**

And afterward,
  I will pour out my Spirit on all people.
Your sons and daughters will prophesy,
  your old men will dream dreams,
  your young men will see visions.
Even on my servants, both men and women,
  I will pour out my Spirit in those days.
I will show wonders in the heavens
  and on the earth,

> blood and fire and billows of smoke.
> The sun will be turned to darkness
>   and the moon to blood
>   before the coming of the great and dreadful day of the LORD.
> And everyone who calls
>   on the name of the LORD will be saved;
> for on Mount Zion and in Jerusalem
>   there will be deliverance,
>   as the LORD has said,
> even among the survivors
>   whom the LORD calls.
>
> **—JOEL 2:28-32**

7. ★ Read some of the Old Covenant promises about the eventual coming of the New Covenant in Jeremiah 31:31-34; Ezekiel 11:19-20; 36:25-27; and Joel 2:28-32.

    Now, without looking at the texts, see how many blessings of the New Covenant you can recall. After brainstorming a list, double-check the texts. Then talk about the implications of each promise of the New Covenant for our lives today.

HUDDLE

8. ★ Name one new thing you are learning . . .

    a. about God

    b. about yourself

9. Prayer option: If time permits and you feel comfortable doing so, take time to pray for one another, that you might hear God's voice this week—through *The End of Religion*, the Bible, prayer, meditation, art, nature, an internal witness, and/or conversations with each other. Invite God's Spirit to speak, and commit to keeping your spiritual ears open.

Session 4

TORAH AND TRADITION
Chapters 9 and 10

HIGHLIGHTS
www.bruxy.com/theendofreligionstudy4

HANG OUT

1. ★ From this session's assigned reading, what stood out to you? Share interesting highlights or lingering questions.
2. In what ways could we say the golden rule is:
   a. universal spiritual teaching?
   b. unique to Jesus?
3. If Jesus liberates his followers from the necessity of rule-keeping, then what is to prevent them from living lives of total anarchy?
4. If the Old Covenant is "obsolete" and the New Covenant is "better," why don't Christians get rid of the Old Testament in their Bibles? (Take a look at 2 Timothy 3:16.)
5. The Bible sometimes speaks positively about tradition, routine, and spiritual habit. What do you think are some positives of tradition and routine? What are some dangers?
6. Recall Jesus' first miracle as discussed in chapter 1. Jesus made a bold symbolic statement at the wedding at Cana when he desecrated the holy water jars with party wine, thereby prioritizing celebration over tradition. If Jesus came

today, what sacred "tradition of the elders" do you think he would need to challenge in contemporary religion in order to make his point?

HEAR

The Pharisees and some of the teachers of the law who had come from Jerusalem gathered around Jesus and saw some of his disciples eating food with hands that were defiled, that is, unwashed. (The Pharisees and all the Jews do not eat unless they give their hands a ceremonial washing, holding to the tradition of the elders. When they come from the marketplace they do not eat unless they wash. And they observe many other traditions, such as the washing of cups, pitchers and kettles.)

So the Pharisees and teachers of the law asked Jesus, "Why don't your disciples live according to the tradition of the elders instead of eating their food with defiled hands?"

He replied, "Isaiah was right when he prophesied about you hypocrites; as it is written:

"'These people honor me with their lips,
     but their hearts are far from me.
They worship me in vain;
     their teachings are merely human rules.'

You have let go of the commands of God and are holding on to human traditions."

And he continued, "You have a fine way of setting aside the commands of God in order to observe your own traditions! For Moses said, 'Honor your father and mother,' and, 'Anyone who curses their father or mother is to be put to death.' But you say that if anyone declares that what might have been used to help their father or mother is Corban (that is, devoted to God)—then you no longer let them do anything for their father or mother. Thus you nullify the word of God by your tradition that you have handed down. And you do many things like that."

Again Jesus called the crowd to him and said, "Listen to me, everyone, and understand this. Nothing outside a person can defile them by going into them. Rather, it is what comes out of a person that defiles them."

After he had left the crowd and entered the house, his disciples asked him about this parable. "Are you so dull?" he asked. "Don't you see that nothing that enters a person from the outside can defile them? For it doesn't go into their heart but into their stomach, and then out of the body." (In saying this, Jesus declared all foods clean.)

He went on: "What comes out of a person is what defiles them. For it is from within, out of a person's heart, that evil thoughts come—sexual immorality, theft, murder, adultery, greed, malice, deceit, lewdness, envy, slander, arrogance and folly. All these evils come from inside and defile a person."

—MARK 7:1-23

7. ★ Read Mark 7:1-23.

   a. ★ What stands out to you from this passage?

   b. ★ The tradition of religious handwashing symbolized that someone wanted to stay separate and uncontaminated from the "sinners" around them. Why would this religious tradition not be appropriate for the followers of Jesus?

   c. In this passage, Jesus first trounces the Pharisees' religious *tradition* on this basis: obeying their oral tradition leads them to disobey what God says in the Torah. Jesus is holding up the Torah, the Law of Moses, as being God's own law that they should have been following. Yet Jesus then goes on to take authority over and terminate the *Torah* itself by declaring all foods clean. What are some implications for Christ-followers living out this multilayered truth—that is, that the Torah is indeed God's own law and yet this law, as law, has now been annulled by Christ?

   d. According to Jesus, sin is not just something bad that you do toward someone, or a systemic structural evil "out there" that makes victims of us all. Sin is an attitude of the heart that we hold toward someone, an attitude which may or may not eventually be expressed through our behavior. We need to get our hearts—and not just our external behaviors, systems, and traditions—right with God (see vv. 6, 19, 21; also see Matthew 5:21-22, 27-28). Why is this approach to human evil—addressing our inner attitudes and not just our externalized behaviors or systematized structures—helpful for our spiritual growth and maximum human flourishing?

8. Bonus Bible bits: Read and discuss Romans 10:4; Colossians 2:8; all of John 5; or all of 2 Corinthians 3.

HUDDLE

9. ★ Name one new thing you are learning . . .

    a. about God
    b. about yourself

10. Jesus said that out of the abundance of the heart the mouth speaks (see Matthew 12:34; Luke 6:45 NRSV). How might you complete this sentence describing your own heart struggles? Some options to get you thinking . . .

    a. Out of the abundance of the heart the hands cheat. (Fudging the truth in documents or tests.)
    b. Out of the abundance of the heart the eyes peep. (Looking at things to covet, or at people in ways that use them rather than bless them.)
    c. Out of the abundance of the heart the feet creep. (Going to places or being with people who are unhealthy for us.)
    d. Out of the abundance of the heart the mouth eats. (Let's move on—this one is far too convicting.)
    e. Out of the abundance of the heart the fingers tweet. (Using social media posts to boost our fragile ego and feed our addiction to affirmation.)
    f. Out of the abundance of the heart the body goes shopping. (Using material things to try to fill an essentially spiritual need.)
    g. Out of the abundance of the heart . . . ?

Session 5

TRIBALISM AND TERRITORY

Chapters 11 and 12

HIGHLIGHTS

www.bruxy.com/theendofreligionstudy5

HANG OUT

1. ★ From this session's assigned reading, what stood out to you? Share interesting highlights or lingering questions.
2. Talk about some examples, global and local, historical and contemporary, of religion trying to mix with politics. What are the recurring results?

HEAR

You have heard that it was said, "Eye for eye, and tooth for tooth." But I tell you, do not resist an evil person. If anyone slaps you on the right cheek, turn to them the other cheek also. And if anyone wants to sue you and take your shirt, hand over your coat as well. If anyone forces you to go one mile, go with them two miles. Give to the one who asks you, and do not turn away from the one who wants to borrow from you.

You have heard that it was said, "Love your neighbor and hate your enemy." But I tell you, love your enemies and pray for those who persecute you, that you may be children of your Father in heaven. He causes his sun to rise on the evil and the good, and sends rain on the righteous and the unrighteous.

—MATTHEW 5:38-45

But to you who are listening I say: Love your enemies, do good to those who hate you, bless those who curse you, pray for those who mistreat you.

—LUKE 6:27-28

Bless those who persecute you; bless and do not curse. Rejoice with those who rejoice; mourn with those who mourn. Live in harmony with one another. Do not be proud, but be willing to associate with people of low position. Do not be conceited.

Do not repay anyone evil for evil. Be careful to do what is right in the eyes of everyone. If it is possible, as far as it depends on you, live at peace with everyone. Do not take revenge, my dear friends, but leave room for God's wrath, for it is written: "It is mine to avenge; I will repay," says the Lord. On the contrary:

"If your enemy is hungry, feed him;
    if he is thirsty, give him something to drink.
In doing this, you will heap burning coals on his head."
Do not be overcome by evil, but overcome evil with good.

—ROMANS 12:14-21

So in Christ Jesus you are all children of God through faith, for all of you who were baptized into Christ have clothed yourselves with Christ. There is neither Jew nor Gentile, neither slave nor free, nor is there male and female, for you are all one in Christ Jesus. If you belong to Christ, then you are Abraham's seed, and heirs according to the promise.

—GALATIANS 3:26-29

3. Read Jesus' teaching on enemy love in the Sermon on the Mount (Matthew 5:38-45).

   a. What stands out to you from this teaching?

   b. Brainstorm: Can you think of any examples of what this principle of enemy love as ethical shock treatment might look like in today's world?

4. ★ Read Luke 6:27-28. Let's dream a little: What effect would it have on the world if a continually growing number of people began to live out this one simple teaching of Jesus? Describe what you imagine the world might gradually become. Be specific.

5. Read Romans 12:14-21. The apostle Paul is helping the early church live out the peace teachings of Jesus. To use a musical analogy, if Jesus is the composer and his teachings are the symphony, then the apostle Paul is the conductor helping the early church play the music well (often with the proficiency of a junior high band).

   a. What parallels/similarities do you see in the teachings of Paul and Jesus?

   b. Paul says Jesus-followers should have no part in "revenge" and "wrath" (judgment and punishment). God will take care of all the judging on judgment day, so we don't have to worry about that. And in the meantime, God will partially work out things like justice and punishment through the government (note that Paul uses the same Greek words for "wrath" and "revenge/punishment" both in 12:19, when he tells Christians to have no part of them, and in 13:4 to describe the role of government). For the early Christians, the roles of the church and the government were decidedly different. This raises the question: To what extent can a Christian who lives by Matthew 5, Luke 6, and Romans 12 participate in the "wrath" and "revenge" of the government in Romans 13? As noted earlier, Christians have historically held two different views:

     i. *Just war*: Christians can wear two hats, living as nonviolent, enemy-loving, peace-promoting, Sermon on the Mount–embodying members of the church when acting as individual Christians or as the church collectively (Romans 12) while also joining with the government to bring justice through violence when acting to represent the state (Romans 13).

    ii. *Peace/pacifism*: Christians cannot wear two hats and are always defined by our identity as Christ-followers, who, like Jesus, love our enemies to death (our death, not theirs) if necessary. We are ambassadors to, rather than citizens of, our earthly kingdoms. And ambassadors to a nation don't get involved in fighting that nation's wars.

So *what do you think?* What might the apostle Paul have had in mind when he first wrote this? What do you think Jesus would say? What side of this debate makes the most sense to you? Try to explain your answer using New Testament teaching of Jesus and the apostles if possible.

6. ★ Read Galatians 3:26-29.

    a. Talk about some of the practical implications of living out this reality today.

    b. How can we meaningfully erase these divisions of race, class, and gender in a way that also retains and celebrates our distinctives and diversity? Talk about some examples.

HUDDLE

7. ★ Name one new thing you are learning . . .

    a. about God

    b. about yourself

8. In the story of the good Samaritan, three attitudes toward material goods are demonstrated:

a. The thieves—"What's yours is mine, and I'm going to get it."

b. The religious leaders—"What's mine is mine, and I'm going to keep it."

c. The Samaritan—"What's mine is yours, and I'm going to share it."

Ask yourself honestly: When do you play the role of each of these in your life?

9. For additional personal reflection: Who is a "Samaritan" to you (not in the sense of being a "good Samaritan," but just a Samaritan, as the term would have meant to a first-century Jew)? In other words, to whom do you feel superior? What person, or kinds of people, or groups of people do you have trouble being in a learning posture toward? (Remember that Jesus not only celebrated the love of the "sinful" Samaritan, but held him up as an example to learn from.) Try to answer with brutal, self-searching honesty. Even if you do not want to feel superior to these people, ask yourself, Whom do I feel superior to? Here are some examples to help jog your imagination:

Conservatives	People of a particular	Cat people
Progressives	race or religion	People who don't like
Rich people	Atheists	pets
Poor people	Young adults	Vegans
Politicians	Children	Meat eaters
Artists	Adult children	Conformists
Capitalists	Therapists	Anarchists
Socialists	People who are in	People who like country
Pacifists	therapy	music
Police officers	People who should be	People who like rap
Criminals	in therapy	music
Feminists	People who put you in	People who prefer talk
Traditionalists	therapy	radio
Homemakers	Ugly people	People who drink
Homewreckers	Attractive people	People who don't drink
The LGBTQ+	Family members	People who drive you
community	Famous people	to drink
The straight community	Loud people	Someone else?
Academic people	Quiet people	
Uneducated people	Dog people	

Session 6

TEMPLE, SYMBOLS, AND SACRIFICE

Chapters 13, 14, and 15

HIGHLIGHTS

www.bruxy.com/theendofreligionstudy6

HANG OUT

1. ★ From this session's assigned reading, what stood out to you? Share interesting highlights or lingering questions.
2. Many church buildings have been designed so that they stand out as especially glorious in their architecture, ornamentation, and art. Consider the following:

    a. What are the possible benefits of this for worshipers?
    b. What are the possible problems it can cause?

3. In your own words, describe why baptism and the eucharist (communion/the Lord's Supper) are *irreligious* practices.
4. What do you think was the multivalent significance of God tearing the curtain of the temple in two at the moment Jesus died on the cross? (I just wanted an excuse to use the word *multivalent*, which is fancy talk for multilayered, many meanings, and multiple applications.)

5. Discuss (if in a group) or think about (if alone) your reaction to the following quote by theologian John Stott:

> Why am I a Christian? One reason is the cross of Christ. Indeed, I could never myself believe in God if it were not for the cross. It is the cross that gives God his credibility. The only God I believe in is the one Nietzsche (the nineteenth-century German philosopher) ridiculed as "God on the cross." In the real world of pain, how could one worship a God who was immune to it?[1]

HEAR

On God showing us his love through the cross . . .

> For God so loved the world that he gave his one and only Son, that whoever believes in him shall not perish but have eternal life. For God did not send his Son into the world to condemn the world, but to save the world through him.
>
> **—JOHN 3:16-17**

> This is how we know what love is: Jesus Christ laid down his life for us. And we ought to lay down our lives for our brothers and sisters.
>
> **—1 JOHN 3:16**

> But God demonstrates his own love for us in this: While we were still sinners, Christ died for us.
>
> **—ROMANS 5:8**

On God saving us from sin through the cross . . .

> Look, the Lamb of God, who takes away the sin of the world!
>
> **—JOHN 1:29B**

For what I received I passed on to you as of first importance: that Christ died for our sins according to the Scriptures.

—1 CORINTHIANS 15:3

Therefore, if anyone is in Christ, the new creation has come: The old has gone, the new is here! All this is from God, who reconciled us to himself through Christ and gave us the ministry of reconciliation: that God was reconciling the world to himself in Christ, not counting people's sins against them. And he has committed to us the message of reconciliation. We are therefore Christ's ambassadors, as though God were making his appeal through us. We implore you on Christ's behalf: Be reconciled to God. God made him who had no sin to be sin for us, so that in him we might become the righteousness of God.

—2 CORINTHIANS 5:17-21

On God setting up his kingdom through the cross . . .

Now is the time for judgment on this world; now the prince of this world will be driven out. And I, when I am lifted up from the earth, will draw all people to myself.

—JOHN 12:31-32

The soldiers twisted together a crown of thorns and put it on his head. They clothed him in a purple robe.

—JOHN 19:2

And they sang a new song, saying:

"You are worthy to take the scroll
and to open its seals,

> because you were slain,
> and with your blood you purchased for God
>   persons from every tribe and language and people
>   and nation.
> You have made them to be a kingdom and priests to serve
>   our God,
>   and they will reign on the earth."
>
> **—REVELATION 5:9-10**

On God shutting down religion through the cross . . .

> For even the Son of Man did not come to be served, but to serve, and to give his life as a ransom for many.
>
> **—MARK 10:45**

> In the same way, after the supper he took the cup, saying, "This cup is the new covenant in my blood, which is poured out for you.
>
> **—LUKE 22:20**

> By calling this covenant "new," he has made the first one obsolete; and what is obsolete and outdated will soon disappear.
>
> **—HEBREWS 8:13**

> I appeal to you therefore, brothers and sisters, by the mercies of God, to present your bodies as a living sacrifice, holy and acceptable to God, which is your spiritual worship.
>
> **—ROMANS 12:1 NRSV**

6. ★ Let's zoom in on the death of Jesus, and what the Bible says are the reasons behind his sacrifice. For each of these points, read the corresponding Scriptures and then try to

summarize the point in your own words. After looking at all four points, talk about the one that resonates with you the most. (Or, divide into four groups and each group study one of the four points. Then come back together to report on what you've learned.)

Jesus died to:

a. *show us* God's love (John 3:16-17; 12:45; 15:13; Romans 5:6-8; 1 John 3:16; 4:10);

b. *save us* from sin (Matthew 9:1-8; John 1:29; 12:46-47; Romans 5:9-10; 1 Corinthians 15:3; 2 Corinthians 5:21; Galatians 1:4; Ephesians 2:5; Colossians 1:21-22; 1 Timothy 1:15; Hebrews 7:27; 9:26; 1 Peter 2:24; 1 John 1:7);

c. *set up* God's kingdom (Matthew 21:1-5; Luke 23:42-43; John 19:19; Revelation 5:9-10; and the ironic symbolism throughout the passion narratives); and

d. *shut down* religion (Mark 10:45; Luke 22:20; Hebrews 8:13; Romans 10:4; 12:1; Ephesians 2:14-15; Colossians 2:13-14; Hebrews 10:17-18).

HUDDLE

7. ★ Name one new thing you are learning . . .

   a. about God

   b. about yourself

8. Read the last two paragraphs on page 188 of *The End of Religion*, starting with "Jesus told his disciples . . ." Talk about your reaction to and experience of this sentence: *If the same Holy Spirit that is in me is also in you, then when we come together we amplify our experience of God.*

Session 7

RESURRECTION AND ASCENSION

Chapters 16 and 17

HIGHLIGHTS

www.bruxy.com/theendofreligionstudy7

HANG OUT

1. ★ From this session's assigned reading, what stood out to you? Share interesting highlights or lingering questions.
2. If you believe in the resurrection and ascension of Jesus, what do you think has convinced you? If you do not believe, what do you think it would take to convince you?

HEAR

> On that day you will realize that I am in my Father, and you are in me, and I am in you.
>
> —JOHN 14:20

What shall we say, then? Shall we go on sinning so that grace may increase? By no means! We are those who have died to sin; how can we live in it any longer? Or don't you know that all of us who were baptized into Christ Jesus were baptized into his death? We were therefore buried with him through baptism into death in order that, just as Christ was raised from the dead through the glory of the Father, we too may live a new life.

For if we have been united with him in a death like his, we will certainly also be united with him in a resurrection like his. For we know that our old self was crucified with him so that the body ruled by sin might be done away with, that we should no longer be slaves to sin—because anyone who has died has been set free from sin.

Now if we died with Christ, we believe that we will also live with him. For we know that since Christ was raised from the dead, he cannot die again; death no longer has mastery over him. The death he died, he died to sin once for all; but the life he lives, he lives to God.

In the same way, count yourselves dead to sin but alive to God in Christ Jesus.

—ROMANS 6:1-11

I have been crucified with Christ and I no longer live, but Christ lives in me. The life I now live in the body, I live by faith in the Son of God, who loved me and gave himself for me.

—GALATIANS 2:20

To them God has chosen to make known among the Gentiles the glorious riches of this mystery, which is Christ in you, the hope of glory.

—COLOSSIANS 1:27

Since, then, you have been raised with Christ, set your hearts on things above, where Christ is, seated at the right hand of God. Set your minds on things above, not on earthly things. For you died, and your life is now hidden with Christ in God. When Christ, who is your life, appears, then you also will appear with him in glory.

—COLOSSIANS 3:1-4

3. ★ The early Christ-followers believed that by entering our world and becoming human, God had somehow bonded his experience to ours and our experience to his. So the early church talked about the death and resurrection and ascension *of Jesus* as also applying *to us*, because they saw us as somehow already being "in Christ." Just as an early Christian might say, "Jesus goes with me in everything I do because Christ is in me," so they might also say, "I go with Jesus in everything he does because I am in Christ." Read the following Bible passages and talk about what it might mean to have "Christ in us" and for us to be "in Christ." Focus on the "so what" for our daily lives, and discuss specific examples of the difference this understanding could make.

   a. John 14:20
   b. Romans 6:1-11
   c. Galatians 2:20
   d. Colossians 1:27
   e. Colossians 3:1-4

HUDDLE

4. ★ Name one new thing you are learning . . .

   a. about God
   b. about yourself

Session 8

WHO WAS (AND IS) JESUS?
Chapters 18, 19, and 20

HIGHLIGHTS
www.bruxy.com/theendofreligionstudy8

HANG OUT

1. ★ From this session's assigned reading, what stood out to you? Share interesting highlights or lingering questions.
2. Do you think God speaks to you? If so, how do you hear God most clearly: through Scripture, nature, the arts, people, circumstances, inner witness (subjective spiritual experiences, like dreams, visions, insights, intuition, or conviction, often enhanced through prayer and meditation)?

HEAR

In the beginning was the Word, and the Word was with God, and the Word was God. He was with God in the beginning. Through him all things were made; without him nothing was made that has been made. In him was life, and that life was the light of all mankind. The light shines in the darkness, and the darkness has not overcome it.

There was a man sent from God whose name was John. He came as a witness to testify concerning that light, so that through him all might believe. He himself was not the light; he came only as a witness to the light.

The true light that gives light to everyone was coming into the world. He was in the world, and though the world was made through him, the world did not recognize him. He came to that which was his own, but his own did not receive him. Yet to all who did receive him, to those who believed in his name, he gave the right to become children of God—children born not of natural descent, nor of human decision or a husband's will, but born of God.

The Word became flesh and made his dwelling among us. We have seen his glory, the glory of the one and only Son, who came from the Father, full of grace and truth.

(John testified concerning him. He cried out, saying, "This is the one I spoke about when I said, 'He who comes after me has surpassed me because he was before me.'") Out of his fullness we have all received grace in place of grace already given. For the law was given through Moses; grace and truth came through Jesus Christ. No one has ever seen God, but the one and only Son, who is himself God and is in closest relationship with the Father, has made him known.

—JOHN 1:1-18

No one has ever seen God; but if we love one another, God lives in us and his love is made complete in us.

—1 JOHN 4:12

Now you are the body of Christ, and each one of you is a part of it.

—1 CORINTHIANS 12:27

3. Read John 1:1-18.

    a. What stands out to you from this passage?

    b. John says in verse 3 that God created the world through the Word. How does this compare with the Genesis account of creation? Where is "the Word" in that story (see Genesis 1:3, 6, 9, 11, 14, 20, 24, 26; Psalm 33:6)?

    c. What do you think John means in verse 9 when he says that Jesus is "the true light that gives light to everyone"?

    d. How does John contrast the Old Covenant (given through Moses) and the New Covenant (given through Jesus)? What are the implications of this?

    e. How do you think John might respond to someone who says, "All religions teach the same truths and show us the same God"?

4. ★ According to John 1:18, 1 John 4:12, and 1 Corinthians 12:27, what is the best way to see God today?

HUDDLE

5. ★ Name one new thing you are learning . . .

    a. about God

    b. about yourself

Session 9

THE WAY OF LOVE

Chapters 21, 22, 23, and 24

HIGHLIGHTS

www.bruxy.com/theendofreligionstudy9

HANG OUT

1. ★ From this session's assigned reading, what stood out to you? Share interesting highlights or lingering questions.
2. Let's brainstorm: Why is the New Covenant "better" than the Old Covenant?
3. The way of law is certainly "safer" if safety is your goal. What are some of the risks of the New Covenant?

HEAR

Dear friends, let us love one another, for love comes from God. Everyone who loves has been born of God and knows God. Whoever does not love does not know God, because God is love. This is how God showed his love among us: He sent his one and only Son into the world that we might live through him. This is love: not that we loved God, but that he loved us and sent his Son as an atoning sacrifice for our sins. Dear friends, since God so loved us, we also ought to love one another. No one has ever seen God; but if we love one another, God lives in us and his love is made complete in us.

This is how we know that we live in him and he in us: He has given us of his Spirit. And we have seen and testify that the Father has sent his Son to be the Savior of the world. If anyone acknowledges that Jesus is the Son of God, God lives in them and they in God. And so we know and rely on the love God has for us.

God is love. Whoever lives in love lives in God, and God in them. This is how love is made complete among us so that we will have confidence on the day of judgment: In this world we are like Jesus. There is no fear in love. But perfect love drives out fear, because fear has to do with punishment. The one who fears is not made perfect in love.

We love because he first loved us. Whoever claims to love God yet hates a brother or sister is a liar. For whoever does not love their brother and sister, whom they have seen, cannot love God, whom they have not seen. And he has given us this command: Anyone who loves God must also love their brother and sister.

—1 JOHN 4:7-21

4. ★ To catch a glimpse of how central love was to the early Christian church, and should be to our lives today, read 1 John 4:7-21.

    a. What stands out to you from this passage?
    b. Jesus introduces the unheard-of irreligious idea that the *primary* way we worship God is by loving others in life-giving ways. (Also see Matthew 25:31-46; John 13:34-35; 14:15, 21, 23; Romans 13:8; Galatians 5:14; James 2:8; 1 Peter 4:8; 1 John 3:16; 2 John 1:6.) So let's brainstorm: What are some different ways that you could have a "worship service" every day this week?

HUDDLE

5. ★ Name one new thing you are learning . . .

    a. about God
    b. about yourself

6. This session's reading addressed how the way of law leads to a loophole mentality. Are there any ethical areas in your life where you are currently investing your energy looking for loopholes rather than following the high standard of love?

Session 10

THE IRRELIGIOUS LIFE
Chapters 25, 26, 27, and Epilogue

HIGHLIGHTS
www.bruxy.com/theendofreligionstudy10

HANG OUT

1. ★ From this session's assigned reading, what stood out to you? Share interesting highlights or lingering questions.
2. What might be the advantages of being a committed member of a healthy, Jesus-following community (the meaning of "church")? List as many as you can.
3. What might be the pitfalls of being part of this same community?
4. What are some things we can do to guard against the pitfalls and maximize the advantages?
5. ★ What, if anything, has *The End of Religion* addressed that could help you on your spiritual journey? What practical steps could you take to live differently in light of this?

HEAR

"Come to me, all you who are weary and burdened, and I will give you rest. Take my yoke upon you and learn from me, for I am gentle and humble in heart, and you will find rest for your souls. For my yoke is easy and my burden is light."

At that time Jesus went through the grainfields on the Sabbath. His disciples were hungry and began to pick some heads of grain and eat them. When the Pharisees saw this, they said to him, "Look! Your disciples are doing what is unlawful on the Sabbath."

He answered, "Haven't you read what David did when he and his companions were hungry? He entered the house of God, and he and his companions ate the consecrated bread—which was not lawful for them to do, but only for the priests. Or haven't you read in the Law that the priests on Sabbath duty in the temple desecrate the Sabbath and yet are innocent? I tell you that something greater than the temple is here. If you had known what these words mean, 'I desire mercy, not sacrifice,' you would not have condemned the innocent. For the Son of Man is Lord of the Sabbath."

—MATTHEW 11:28–12:8

6. ★ Read Matthew 11:28–12:8.

   a. ★ What stands out to you from this passage?

   b. Jesus points back to two examples of love overriding law in the Old Testament:

      i. King David seemed to know God's heart enough to break God's law whenever it would lead to more love. He and his men ate the sacred bread of the tabernacle, something that was for only the priests to eat (see 1 Samuel 21:1-6).

      ii. The same law that commanded every Israelite must not work on the Sabbath also commanded priests to work on the Sabbath. Obviously, says Jesus, even the Law should not be taken legalistically. God's character of love over law was always at work behind the scenes, for those who had ears to hear and eyes to see.

      How do these two examples help us understand what Jesus is getting at when he references Hosea 6:6, "I desire mercy, not sacrifice"?

    c. ★ What do you need most from Jesus these days? Rest from your burdens? Purpose and direction (the yoke/ teaching of Jesus)? Something else? Reflect back over the past ten sessions and talk about what you will be taking with you from this time of learning.

HUDDLE

7. ★ Name one new thing you are learning . . .

    a. about God

    b. about yourself

Bonus Chapter 1

THE FAITH INSTINCT

I have been tortured with longing to believe ... and the yearning grows stronger the more cogent the intellectual difficulties that stand in the way.

—Fyodor Dostoyevsky

Jesus never used the word *religion* to describe God's goal for his spiritual family. Instead, Jesus used the word *faith*, which is a relational concept that points toward a committed connection between persons. Faith, in the biblical languages of Hebrew (Old Testament) and Greek (New Testament), means trust and trustworthiness, believing faithfulness, and active allegiance. This relational orientation called "faith" is what we were made for.

THE UNIVERSALITY OF SPIRITUALITY

The famed biologist E. O. Wilson, known as "the father of sociobiology," said that "the predisposition to religious belief is the most complex and powerful force in the human mind and in all probability an ineradicable part of human nature."[1] The Bible teaches that human beings were built for belief; that is, for a trusting relationship with the One who not only made us, but made us godlike.

Unfortunately, humans have mistakenly diverted our God-given trust instinct into the rules, rituals, and representations of our own creation: a phenomenon the Bible calls "idolatry" (see Romans 1:18-25).

We are wired to believe in the transcendent—something beyond ourselves that gives our lives meaning and value—and we express that belief with, among other things, organized ritual. Anthropologists tell us that all people groups throughout history, universally and independent of each other, have exhibited some sort of faith instinct.

Consider what may be the world's oldest known architecture: the temple at Göbekli Tepe in southern Turkey, which is estimated to have been built by hunter-gatherers during the earliest days of the Neolithic period, starting around approximately 9600 BC.[2] This religious structure used for corporate worship not only predates Stonehenge and the Egyptian pyramids; it predates any known long-term human settlements. Before writing or the wheel, before we settled down into cities, societies, and civilizations, human beings were worshipers. In light of this and other discoveries, theories are shifting: Anthropologists used to assume that humans built religious structures, like temples, after they settled into permanent places and created more fixed societies. Organized religion evolved, it was believed, out of stable societies. But now the evidence suggests it might be the other way around—we stopped being nomads because we found certain sites sacred, and we decided to stay.

This universal awareness of something beyond the physical realm goes back even further, to the very dawn of our species, *Homo sapiens*, and even includes our cousins the Neanderthals. Writing about a Neanderthal practice from about one hundred thousand years ago, author Karen Armstrong reports, "Archaeologists have unearthed Neanderthal graves containing weapons, tools and the bones of a sacrificed animal, all of which suggest some kind of belief in a future world that was similar to their own."[3] Armstrong also points out that in at least some Neanderthal graves, the corpse seems to have been deliberately placed in a fetal position, as though being prepared for rebirth.[4] Although we may never know the specifics of Neanderthal beliefs, we can at least deduce that they were, in fact, believers. This is also true for what we know about the earliest members of our species: from the earliest known human cultures, those we call *Homo sapiens* have also been *Homo religiosus*.[5]

"*Homo sapiens* have had spiritual beliefs since the dawn of our species," writes Dean Hamer in *The God Gene: How Faith Is Hardwired into Our Genes*. "Spirituality is one of our basic human inheritances. It is, in fact, an instinct." Hamer goes on to quote William James: "It is as if there were in the human consciousness a *sense of reality, a feeling of objective presence, a perception* of what we may call 'something there,' more deep and more general than any of the special and particular 'senses.'"[6]

As humans, we have an urge, an instinct, an impulse to move emotionally, relationally, and even ritualistically toward something beyond ourselves. We feel called toward this force that is our Source and our Goal, the One we have come from and are searching for. In the words of philosopher Martin Buber, we crave an "I-Thou" relationship with Ultimate Reality.

This kind of faith is neither caught nor taught; it simply is. Across every culture, throughout all ages, people have exhibited a naturally occurring, intuitive belief—an impulse to connect which is as universal and natural as breathing. Humans experience this faith instinct in many ways, of which I will mention three: the God-impulse, the eternity-impulse, and the ethical-impulse.

THE GOD-IMPULSE

By "God-impulse" I'm referring to the universal intuition that there is some Ultimate Reality beyond or embedded within our material universe. Usually this Ultimate Reality is thought of as personal, conscious, even relational in some way. This Ultimate Reality is what most human cultures have called God or the gods.

To be clear, I'm not suggesting that actual belief or faith in God is universal—only the *impulse* to believe. What we do with that impulse is a human choice, and this accounts for the existence, though a minority throughout history, of nonbelievers.

I remember hearing popular and prolific anti-theist writer Christopher Hitchens talk about his own God-impulse in a radio interview. He described his personal instinctive, reflexive, intuitive hunch that there is some personality at work in his life beyond himself. Especially, he said, when extreme coincidences happen, he feels like there is "something more" out there involved in the circumstances of his life. But then, as an intelligent, informed, twenty-first-century human, he is able to explain and attribute those impulses to other psychological mechanisms. The human instinct to believe is, according to Hitchens, a kind of evolutionary holdover that may once have been beneficial, but has long since outlived its usefulness, similar to but more dangerous than a vestigial body part, like the human tailbone, wisdom teeth, and male nipples.

An increasing amount of evidence suggests that even though we tend to believe specific things because of our upbringing (*nurture*), our *impulse* to believe in Something or Someone beyond ourselves is a natural, fundamental aspect of our humanity (*nature*). This is similar to language acquisition—people are born with innate instincts for learning language. Understanding and communicating through verbal expression happens without trying (unlike reading and writing). What language we learn will depend on our culture and family, but the *instinct* and *ability* to relate, connect, and communicate through language is in us from birth. We can debate why this is the case, but the fact is that for humans, the impulse to believe in a reality beyond our physical world is intuitive and universal.

This God-impulse may manifest first as an awe-impulse: our sense of wonder at something bigger than and beyond ourselves. This awe-impulse can be found in the sense of vertigo we experience while lying under the stars at night and contemplating the infinite nature of the universe. It can be found in the tears that well up in our eyes the first time we see magnificent mountains or experience the expansive grandeur of places like Victoria Falls.

I remember talking with a young Jewish woman who told me the story of how she came to believe in Jesus one December while listening to Handel's *Messiah*. Her experience was sub-cognitive, pure awe. She began listening as a nonbeliever and somewhere in the middle of the "Hallelujah Chorus," she was so filled with a sense of numinous awe that she found herself believing that the one who is the inspiration for this music is the center of everything.

Theologian John Stott writes, "We know instinctively that there is a transcendent reality beyond the material order, and people are seeking it everywhere." We sense that there is "something else, something more, something awesome that no scientific instrument is able to apprehend or measure."[7]

Anabaptist theologian Scot McKnight agrees that "there is something in each human being that reaches out for God, and that reaching instinct comes from God and leads to God." He calls this our "aching for deity."[8]

The Bible says that this impulse for something more, something beyond ourselves, something we feel called to move toward with all our heart, arises from deep within the human psyche and is, at the same time, heightened and confirmed by our surroundings. The apostle Paul writes, "For since the creation of the world God's invisible qualities—his eternal power and divine nature—have been clearly seen, being understood from what has been made, so that people are without excuse" (Romans 1:20). About the beauty of our world, philosopher C. S. Lewis writes:

> We do not want merely to see beauty, though, God knows, even that is bounty enough. We want something else which can hardly be put into words—to be united with the beauty we see, to pass into it, to receive it into ourselves, to bathe in it, to become part of it. . . . At present we are on the outside of the world, the wrong side of the door. We discern the freshness and purity of morning, but they do not make us fresh and pure. We cannot mingle with the splendours we see.[9]

It is no accident that sex feels transcendent, that orgasm seems to transport us beyond ourselves, that intercourse or masturbation reflects a desire not just to escape but to connect, and that temple prostitution was standard practice in many ancient religions. G. K. Chesterton is rumored to have said, "A man knocking on the door of a brothel is looking for God."[10]

Everything inside and outside us invites us on a journey toward something we cannot describe. The wonderful thinker Huston

Smith points out that this intuition creates a dissatisfaction that in turn may generate a spiritual quest:

> There is within us—in even the blithest, most lighthearted among us—a fundamental dis-ease. . . . This desire lies in the marrow of our bones and deep in the regions of our soul. All great literature, poetry, art, philosophy, psychology, and religion tries to name and analyze this longing. We are seldom in direct touch with it, and indeed the modern world seems set on preventing us from getting in touch with it by covering it with . . . entertainments, obsessions, and distractions of every sort. But the longing is there, built into us like a jack-in-the-box that presses for release. . . . Whether we realize it or not, simply to be human is to long for release from mundane existence with its confining walls of finitude and morality. The Good News . . . is that that longing can be fulfilled.[11]

The story of Neo in the classic sci-fi movie *The Matrix* may be the story of every one of us. Although he must be educated by others to see the true reality, what Neo learns resonates with what he has always known. Neo's mentor, Morpheus, tells him, "Let me tell you why you're here. You're here because you know something. What you know you can't explain, but you feel it. You've felt it your entire life."[12]

This feeling is our feeling. Like a child learning to talk, we were built with this capacity—we just need help from others to give us the words.

Intuitively, we not only believe that there is something more out there, but also believe that we need this something more, that this mysterious "more" has something to tell us, to show us, to give us—something that might solve our problem and rescue us from our less-than-complete human experience.

In the words of the great Jewish social psychologist Erich Fromm, "There is no one without a religious need, a need to have a frame of orientation and an object of devotion. . . . The question is not religion or not, but which kind of religion."[13] So we arrive at the same conclusion as psychologist Justin Barret, who writes that "belief in God is an almost inevitable consequence of the kind of minds we have."[14]

The human God-impulse is *axiomatic*—it is a basic belief, self-evident knowledge arising out of our intuition. It is not something we argue ourselves into believing. Our God-impulse is simply there, although we may argue ourselves *out* of believing it. Those who successfully deny their own God-impulse create alternate theories to explain it away, but the experience of it is universal, even if the explanation differs. To be human is to have the creative capacity to talk ourselves out of or completely repress what is a fundamental universal human experience. But I am convinced that, at the deepest levels of our being, we know there is Something More.

I have sometimes heard skeptics ask a person of faith why they believe in God, as though theism is an unusual human oddity that must be explained by factors such as parental influence, cultural conditioning, or emotional neediness. But the evidence from history, anthropology, psychology, and even current neuroscience suggests the opposite.[15] To be drawn toward faith in God is to be a normal, functioning human being, in tune with our history and our hardwiring. Instead, it is atheism that qualifies as the unusual human oddity toward which some humans reason themselves.

THE TRUTH WE KNOW WE KNOW

We all live life with "basic beliefs," or "intuitive beliefs." In the world of mathematics and logic, these basic beliefs are called *axioms*. Axioms are self-evident concepts. They are not arrived at through reason or logic. Once pointed out, they are simply seen to be true in and of themselves. For instance, the *axiom of equals* reads like this:

If A = B
and C = B
then A = C

There is no formula to prove this statement. It is a basic belief. It is used to prove other theories, but nothing can "prove" it. The axiom of equals is simply known. It is intuitive knowledge, basic belief, self-evident reality.

Self-evident knowledge is powerful. It becomes the foundation for all other forms of knowing because it is not based on research, data, evidence, or formulas. Axiomatic knowledge is bedrock to our soul—*the truth we know we know.*

Perhaps this is why the writers of the American Declaration of Independence began it with the words "We hold these truths to be self-evident . . ." It is an invitation to search within your own heart and to join them in admitting what you already know to be true: all people are created with equal value and dignity. (Unfortunately, many of the framers of this declaration at the time owned humans as property, whom they did not consider equal, and women were denied the right to vote. Our personal prejudices can create powerful blind spots.) Imagine if the same document were crafted with a top ten list of evidence to prove the points it asserts. Would that make it a more powerful statement? No, quite the contrary. People would end up arguing about the validity of the evidence rather than seeing and accepting the axiomatic truth, the truth we know we know: all people are ultimately equal and infinitely worthy.

In our search for an answer to the question of whether God exists, we can either pursue a rationalistic course and debate the various evidences for the existence of a deity or take a more intuitive approach and consider whether God is axiomatic to our soul. Does the human God-impulse speak to the "self-evident" truth that we were meant for something more—a relationship with Someone greater than ourselves? Or is there some other explanation for it?

Philosopher Dallas Willard offers his opinion: "Human beings have always known there is a God, and they have understood to some degree what he is like (Romans 1:19-20)." Willard is referring to that passage in the Bible that says our own internal instinct to believe in God is reinforced by what we see and experience externally all around us. The world is spectacular in its artistry, pointing our hearts toward the Divine Artist.[16]

So if you have ever wondered whether you think about God and other spiritual realities only because you happened to be born into a culture that introduced you to the concepts, you don't have to wonder anymore. The evidence of history, psychology, anthropology, and neuroscience suggests that you think about God because you are compelled to. You are hardwired for God. It is part of being human. Also, part of being human is the choice to explain away our God-impulse, as some individuals and societies have done, but the impulse itself is an elemental ingredient in human nature.

THE ETERNITY-IMPULSE
Our impulse toward God also expresses itself as an immortality-impulse. We feel that we should live forever. Death feels unnatural. Life cries out for a sequel.

Have you ever been at a funeral and just thought to yourself, "This is weird. Life is not supposed to do this, to stop." When someone dies, most of us habitually find ways to talk about that person continuing on, even if that is just in our memories. We say things like "They will always live on in our hearts," whatever that means. When we have experienced a loving connection with someone in the present, it feels wrong to leave that person entirely in the past. Or maybe you have found yourself contemplating your own death, and thought to yourself, "No way. This whole idea just isn't right." The atheist thinker Robert Buckman writes, "The desire for immortality is an unfathomably deep urge—so deep and powerful and primal that it can best be considered as a basic component of the human psyche."[17] If you are human, then something inside you feels strongly that you should live forever. Why is that?

King Solomon, the ancient ruler known for his wisdom (he was sometimes called the wisest man who ever lived, but I think that title should go to Jesus), theorized in his most philosophical work that God has somehow "set eternity in the human heart" (Ecclesiastes 3:11). In other words, it seemed to Solomon that human beings are wired to live forever with God. We have been fitted with a kind of spiritual homing mechanism to guide us toward our true home with the divine. Solomon is pointing to the origin of Buckman's "basic component of the human psyche"—the desire for immortality. If not God, then what is the source of this impulse toward the infinite?

To my mind, atheistic evolution alone does not provide a compelling answer to the origin of our eternity-impulse. According to the theory of evolution, human desire evolved in relationship to corresponding fulfillments of that desire. We grow hungry because we need to eat, we get thirsty because we must drink, we desire sex because we should perpetuate the species. But why evolve such a strong and consistent desire for, and expectation of, an afterlife if the whole instinct and idea is bogus? If there is no God, and if life ends with our last physical breath, then the universally human eternity-impulse is maladaptive to our environment, and as an increasing number of authors have suggested, it is a potentially self-destructive force. After all, it is belief in the rewards of an afterlife that continues to motivate suicide terrorism and other religious evils around the world today.

Author Mark Tabb points to a better explanation for our eternity-impulse:

> "The presence of the image of God within us is why we long for something we cannot find in the world in which we live. When God made us like Himself, He placed a longing for the eternal—that which is permanent—deep within our souls. We're like God in that our frame of reference can never be confined to the physical universe."[18]

THE ETHICAL-IMPULSE

Let's look at one last axiomatic impulse beyond the God-impulse and the eternity-impulse that points to a reality beyond ourselves—the ethical-impulse. People often speak of "human rights" as though there should be some universally understood and accepted value placed on every individual human being and therefore a universally understood and accepted human ethic. We intuit the intrinsic value of human life. But where does this impulse come from? Why should we think that humans have innate inalienable rights any more than the ants we step on, or the grass we mow, or the bacteria we kill off with our antibiotics?[19]

For some reason, most people groups intuit that it is morally, objectively wrong to kill people the way we kill germs. Why is that? Is it merely because we think it is inconsistent to kill our own kind? Is our desire to preserve human life mere speciesism? We are horrified at individuals and groups of people, like Hitler and the Nazis of World War II, who justify the mass extermination of other humans like rodents. And our horror is not just emotional repulsion, but involves deep moral rejection of the act, like a body throwing up after ingesting some tainted food: we reject these acts as objectively, intrinsically, ethically unacceptable. They are wrong.[20]

This ethical instinct points to the One in whose image we are created. The apostle Paul talks about God implanting his own ethical "law" inside all people to guide them, even if they have never heard of the Ten Commandments, read the Bible, or studied the Sermon on the Mount. This God-given guidance happens through the conviction of what we call a *conscience*. Of course, we are all aware of narcissists, sociopaths, and psychopaths who have a greatly diminished ability to empathize with others.[21] Their conscience is compromised, but not completely absent. Just try to hold a harmful narcissist accountable for their hurtful behavior and they will likely protest the injustice done toward *them*. A sense of right and wrong is present, but is distorted, contorted, bent in on itself. And many who are technically sociopaths live moral lives—lives based not on their inner impulse of conscience but on strong ethical conviction.[22] This doesn't negate the idea of God's design for human conscience, it merely points to how a good design can be and has been twisted, abused, and sometimes entirely broken.

In the apostle Paul's words,

> "The Gentiles do not have the Law; but whenever they do by instinct what the Law commands, they are their own law, even though they do not have the Law. Their conduct shows that what the Law commands is written in their hearts. Their consciences also show that this is true, since their thoughts sometimes accuse them and sometimes defend them" (Romans 2:14-15 GNT).

God has written "what the Law commands" on the human heart because we are all made in God's ethical image. I find that religious people are sometimes surprised to meet genuinely moral and caring people who have a different faith or no faith at all. They seem suspicious of anyone who has a strong ethical life apart from faith in God. In Protestant circles, this is likely because of the influence of the doctrine of "total depravity," a belief that sin has penetrated and corrupted every area of human life. Taken to its extreme, total depravity negates the divine image-bearing beauty of being human. In his commentary on Genesis, Protestant Reformer John Calvin wrote that "the image of God had been destroyed in us by the fall" and then goes on to try to justify this patently unbiblical statement: "But now, although some obscure lineaments of that image are found remaining in us; yet are they so vitiated and maimed, that they may truly be said to be destroyed."[23] Martin Luther, also in his commentary on Genesis, commented: "I am afraid that *since the loss of this image through sin* we cannot understand it to any extent. Memory, will, and mind we have indeed; but they are most depraved and most seriously weakened, yes, to put it more clearly, they are utterly leprous and unclean."[24] And so, Protestant theology teaches that the image of God in us is so "utterly leprous and unclean" and so "perverted and maimed" that it is almost unrecognizable, a kind of near-non-reality. This way of thinking effectively neutralizes the power and potency of what the Bible actually says.

The Bible is unequivocal on this fact: all humans are made in the image of a moral God (Genesis 1:26-27), and this image is fully a part of every human's identity even after sin enters the picture (Genesis 9:6; 1 Corinthians 11:7; James 3:9). We can therefore expect high morality among all kinds of people regardless of religious or ideological affiliation (the point of Romans 2:14-15, above). It is a biblical belief to anticipate high moral standards from all humans across all cultures and belief systems. In other words, moral, loving, life-affirming atheists are evidence not against but in favor of a biblical worldview.

And when humans follow this inner, intuitive moral compass, we feel the nourishment of our own authenticity. Augustine wrote in his *Confessions*, "You have made us for yourself, and our heart is restless until it rests in you."[25]

LISTENING TO OUR INTUITIONS

There is a reality that we arrive at not through language or mathematics, but only through experience. We know it is true because we sense it, not because we are *told* it is true, and not because we *reason* it is true, as though proving a mathematical formula.

Although a man may technically become a father at the biological moment of his child's conception, he emotionally and relationally becomes a father the moment he holds his newborn child, in an ecstatic state, beyond words, where only tears are adequate to express his experience. This bonding experience is real. Neuroscientists tell us that something different, measurable, neurological happens at that moment—a neural attachment is formed in a father's brain that can be detected through brain imaging tests.[26] Something is more true in this moment than all the words in all the books on parenting ever written. And we know this. Our intuition tells us so. And that same intuition is also telling us God is real.

C. S. Lewis again, at length:

> The Christian says, "Creatures are not born with desires unless satisfaction for those desires exists. A baby feels hunger: well, there is such a thing as food. A duckling wants to swim: well, there is such a thing as water. Men feel sexual desire: well, there is such a thing as sex. If I find in myself a desire which no experience in this world can satisfy, the most probable explanation is that I was made for another world. If none of my earthly pleasures satisfy it, that does not prove that the universe is a fraud. Probably earthly pleasures were never meant to satisfy it, but only to arouse it, to suggest the real thing. If that is so, I must take care, on the one hand, never to despise, or to be unthankful for, these earthly blessings, and on the other, never to mistake them for the something else of which they are only a kind of copy, or echo, or mirage. I must keep alive in myself the desire for my true country, which I shall not find till after death; I must never let it get snowed

under or turned aside; I must make it the main object of life to press on to that country and to help others to do the same."[27]

This brings us full circle to King Solomon's theory—that humans reach out for the eternal because they are designed to do so by a higher power. We are hardwired for God by God. We are built with an internal homing mechanism, an implanted desire that corresponds with Ultimate Reality.

Again, C. S. Lewis sums it up best when he says:

> Our lifelong nostalgia, our longing to be reunited with something in the universe from which we now feel cut off, our desire to be on the inside of a door which we have always seen from the outside: this is no mere neurotic fancy, but the truest index of our real situation.[28]

KNOW GOD. NO RELIGION.

Are we made for religion? No. We are made for God. There is a difference. While praying to the Father, Jesus said, "Now this is eternal life: that they know you, the only true God, and Jesus Christ, whom you have sent" (John 17:3). Life is found not in the traditions and systems of religion but in the "knowing"— the firsthand, experiential intimacy with the Almighty that God makes possible for us through Jesus. This *knowing* is what Jesus summarizes through his regular use of the word *faith*, which means *trust*—the foundation for any meaningful relationship.

Religion, then, is the result of a malfunctioning faith instinct. In the words of philosopher Paul Davies, "Religions represent an attempt to harness innate spirituality for organizational purposes."[29] It sublimates our God-impulse into an institutional codependency.

Canada geese have an instinct to fly south for the winter. Humans have an instinct to relate to God. Human religion is like geese holding conferences, drawing flowcharts, and deciding on authority structures for their flight path. None of this actually gets anybody anywhere.

I am not writing any of this to convince you that God is real. I am convinced that in your heart of hearts, you are already convinced. I am sharing these thoughts to invite you to listen to what your own heart is telling you. And to compare what you hear within to what Jesus has been saying for two thousand years. When we compare our internal intuitions with the external reality of the teachings and example of Jesus that we read about in the Bible and see in the lives of his people, a spiritual spark ignites, because we are hearing God in stereo.

Bonus Chapter 2

THE ORIGIN OF RELIGION

Remoteness from God is not a matter of physical distance,
but a spiritual problem of relationship.
—Rabbi Adin Steinsaltz, *The Thirteen Petalled Rose*

Do you sometimes feel that you have to do something to make God like you? Does the idea of God knowing everything about you make you feel anxious? Or does God knowing you completely give you a sense of assurance and security? If you had to rate the intimacy versus distance between you and God—with 5 being a "best friends" level of closeness, and 1 being a "stranger on the other side of the street" level of closeness—where would you place yourself? Depending on how you answer these questions, you may suffer from a psycho-spiritual disease called SSA—that is, spiritual separation anxiety.

SPIRITUAL SEPARATION ANXIETY

SSA is the root of religion and the soil out of which sin grows. Here's how it works: First we buy into the belief that God is distant, disinterested, detached, or maybe even disappointed in us. For whatever reason, God is withholding his life and love from us. Then, out of our conscious or subconscious panic, we take it upon ourselves to bridge the perceived God gap. We beg from, barter with, or build bridges to God through religious ritual. Or we run in what appears to be the opposite direction, seeking life and love from other sources that we use as God-surrogates. Yet the whole enterprise is misguided, because God hasn't gone anywhere. We don't need to build a stairway to heaven or a Tower of Babel to reach God. God is with us, all around us, always moving us to notice and to receive God's love.

So how did we get so far off track? How did the human species move from faith to fear, from relational spirituality to anxiety-ridden religion? As in the biblical story of Jacob and Esau, when did humankind exchange the spiritual security of our precious birthright for a cheap bowl of bland stew? Why did we sell out and buy in to a system that preys upon and exacerbates our SSA? Where did it all start?

To answer these questions, we're going back to the beginning. The very beginning.

BANG

And it all began. Out of nothing came everything. Or so they say. Except, what power, what force, what concept, what reality can generate that kind of shift from nothingness to thingness, from nonmatter to matter, from nonbeing to being, from nonexistence to existence? Theoretical physicist Stephen Hawking once wrote, "Because there is a law such as gravity, the universe can and will create itself from nothing. Spontaneous creation is the reason there is something rather than nothing, why the universe exists, why we exist."[1] I don't like being on the other side of any debate with the mind of Stephen Hawking, but it seems to me that he didn't back up the bus of history quite far enough. We're not talking about the law of gravity creating the universe; we're talking about *nothing* creating the law of gravity, and everything else. In the words of Shakespeare's King Lear, "Nothing will come of nothing."

The kind of sudden, complete shift in the nature of reality described by the "big bang" suggests the presence of the power of choice. Pure will. Absolute mind. The big bang requires a Big Banger. Before the physical universe existed, the realm of will, choice, and decision was the base reality. *Mind preceded matter.*

That Mind is what we call "God," and that God is what the Bible calls "Love" (1 John 4:8, 16).[2]

God is love. To utter those three beautiful words is to say that the base reality of everything is not only personal, but relational. God is an absolute energy of engagement. Evangelist Glen Scrivener writes, "And here's what it means. For all eternity there was give-and-take, back-and-forth. There was friendliness. Therefore God is not defined by supremacy but by sharing."[3] This is where we all came from. It is the nature of love to expand rather than shrink away, to give rather than restrict, to create rather than destroy, and to invite rather than reject. And so God creates us and invites us into relationship with God's own self.

Keep in mind, this Absolute-Energy-of-Engagement is what the Bible means when it says "God." The Bible begins with the words "In the beginning God created" (Genesis 1:1).[4] And there it is: Mind before matter; Love before anything else.

BEING GODLIKE

What is clear in the Bible is that God wanted to go beyond making pets to making people—beings like God. A global petting zoo was never God's goal for planet Earth. God always intended to make animals who were more than animals. So later in the first chapter of Genesis we read some of the most profound words ever written:

> And God said, "Let us make humankind in our image and according to our likeness, and let them rule over the fish of the sea, and over the birds of heaven, and over the cattle, and over all the earth, and over every moving thing that moves upon the earth." So God created humankind in his image, in the likeness of God he created him, male and female he created them. (Genesis 1:26-27 LEB)[5]

This is a new thought on the face of the planet. Researcher and author Lois Tverberg writes:

> Mythologies in the ancient Near East portrayed humans as the slaves of cruel, capricious, callous gods, created so that the gods could enjoy leisure. A pessimism haunted ancient

writings that life was worthless and futile. Homer lamented, "This is the lot the gods have spun for miserable men, that they should live in pain; yet themselves are sorrowless."

In much of the ancient world, life was cheap. Historians estimate that if you lived in a tribal society, your chances of dying a violent death at the hands of someone else were about one in six, because war, slavery, and barbaric cruelty were shockingly commonplace.[6]

But the creation story at the beginning of the Hebrew Bible changes all of this. Other ancient Near Eastern creation myths, like the Babylonian *Enuma Elish*, taught that only kings and queens were made in the image of the gods. In these creation stories, humans were made by the gods to be the gods' slaves, to do their bidding and to serve them food. But in the Bible, the one true God makes us all godlike, and *God* is the one who gives *humans* food in the garden of Eden. This is revolutionary—and dangerous.

This kind of thinking—thinking that elevates all people to friends of God, partners with God in taking care of the planet, and representatives of God to each other and the world around us as God's image bearers—is potentially disruptive to slavery-based societies and power-based religions. This deep truth promotes all people to something more than puppets, more than marionettes moved by the hands of heaven, playing out the prescribed script of a sovereign Puppet Master. No, we humans are infinitely precious and powerfully creative, divine-like beings.

In her insightful book *The Very Good Gospel*, advocate, activist, and author Lisa Sharon Harper writes about the implications of this unprecedented teaching on the value and dignity of every single human being:

> *All humanity is made in the image of God.* To slap another human is to slap the image of God. To lie to another human is to lie to the image of God. To exploit another human is to exploit the image of God. To kill another human is to kill the image of God. To declare war on another human or an ethnic group or a religion or a nation is to declare war on the image of God. In essence, to commit acts of physical, emotional, psychological,

sexual, political, and economic violence against fellow humans is to attempt to crush the image of God on earth.[7]

Getting back to the biblical text, did you notice that in Genesis 1:26-27 above, when God creates humankind, God speaks to God's own self in the plural ("Let *us* make humankind in *our* image and according to *our* likeness")? This is so important if we want to understand the story of human origin, human purpose, and human destiny. We've already talked about the three beautiful words—"God is love" (1 John 4:8, 16)—which means that God is always eternally and infinitely relational. God is always engaged in loving relationship within Godself. And this has totalizing implications for us as God's image bearers. We were made in God's image and likeness—made by Love for love, by Relationship for relationship. All people are equally made to be like God, in God's image. Every one of us human beings finds absolute value and infinite worth in our identity as an image bearer of God. For humans to be godlike means that we are inherently ethical, creatively powerful, and absolutely relational. We have the moral capacity for genuine goodness, the creative capacity to shape the future history of the planet, and the spiritual capacity for intimate relationship with God and one another.

TO SERVE AND PROTECT

Also notice in the opening chapters of Genesis that humans are given a kind of power and responsibility that other animals are not: humans are told to "fill the earth and subdue it" and to "rule over" all of creation (Genesis 1:28). This is the original great commission given by God to humankind. What this "ruling over" the world will look like is made clearer in the second chapter of Genesis, where it says that we rule by "serving" and "protecting" all of creation (see Genesis 2:15).

The motto of the Toronto police force is To Serve and Protect. And that is what the Bible says all humans are called to do for one another and all of creation.

It is good for us to admit and embrace this power and responsibility. Real damage to the planet can happen when we assume our rulership should be self-serving or, equally, when we ignore our uniqueness that sets us apart from the rest of the animal kingdom. For instance, the choices humans make will influence the lives of dolphins more than dolphin decisions will influence the lives of humans. That dynamic is by design, and we should admit our failure to be Earth's caretakers as we were created to be.[8]

The first chapter of Genesis says we were made to move into the world to "fill the earth and subdue it" (1:28). Then in the second chapter of Genesis, God places humankind in a garden for us to learn how to serve and protect (2:15), before moving us out into the world. The garden was our training ground.

We (and notice I'm using *we* language, because I think the story of Adam and Eve is the story of us all, with universal lessons to teach us[9]) began our life with God having been given all the food, shelter, friendship, and purpose we need to live an abundant life. And this includes the possibility of choice, for true love necessitates choice.

For us to become the choice-making, love-embracing image bearers we were made to be, God decided to give us a clear choice. God tells Adam that there is a way we could walk away from God and choose our own independence, our own way forward, if that is what we choose: we could eat from "the tree of the knowledge of good and evil" (Genesis 2:17).[10] God warns us that this will lead us away from God and therefore toward death, since God is the source and sustainer of life. And at first, all seems to be going swimmingly. Adam and Eve are "naked and unashamed" (see Genesis 2:25), enjoying intimacy with each other, with all creation, and with our Creator. But then . . .

A SNAKE IN THE GRASS

To call the devil "a snake in the grass" is an insult to snakes, and to grass. But serpents do make for an effective symbol of Satan. Snakes are silent as they slither, they are potentially poisonous, and they attack from below. And so, at the start of Genesis 3, Satan makes his first appearance in the Bible, in the form of a serpent:[11]

Now the serpent was more crafty than any of the wild animals the LORD God had made. He said to the woman, "Did God really say, 'You must not eat from any tree in the garden'?" (Genesis 3:1)

If you look closely, you will see a truckload of truth driving right up your nose through this one verse. Note that the serpent (who we later learn is the devil himself) is not described as more powerful or horrific or even evil, but as "crafty" (Heb. *arum*)—a word that means subtle, sensible, and shrewd (translated "prudent" in Proverbs). The word refers to the power to read people and situations and move them in a desired direction. Now catch this: When partnered with loving character, we call this skill insight, wisdom, and good leadership. But apart from love, the same skill will manifest in selfish manipulation. And with this warning, the author of Genesis invites us to open our eyes to see the serpent's wily ways in what happens next. Jewish scholar Ziony Zevit writes: "By describing the serpent as *arum*, the Iron Age author signaled, *Caveat lector! Caveat auditor!* Reader, beware! Listener, beware! Attend carefully to the use and misuse of language in the story that is about to follow. Scrutinize closely what is said and what is omitted."[12] And when we follow these instructions, we see Satan's sneaky strategies unfold in three ways:

First, the serpent engages Eve, not Adam, even though Adam is apparently present alongside Eve. This is significant. For some reason, Satan sees Eve as the easier target, someone more open to suggestion and confusion. For centuries, religious authorities and church leaders have appealed to the serpent's targeting Eve and Eve's poor performance in the interaction as the reason why women should not be religious leaders. Women in general, they say, must be more easily deceived and led astray.

But the Bible suggests a different reason for the serpent choosing Eve as his mark. From Genesis 2 we learn that Eve was not yet created out of Adam when God gave Adam the instruction not to eat from the tree of the knowledge of good and evil. The narrator has compressed events and leaves us to assume that God trusted Adam to then pass this instruction along to Eve (which

is in keeping with God's commitment to do things in partnership with God's image bearers as seen throughout the rest of the
Bible). Now, we all know that it is easier to disorient and manip-
ulate someone who has only secondhand knowledge of any topic,
especially spiritual realities, rather than someone who has learned
and experienced things for themselves.[13] Sure enough, Eve's partial knowledge and secondhand information becomes evident in
her confusion as the conversation unfolds.

Second, the serpent begins with a question. This is the first
recorded question in the Bible, and it is no ordinary question: it
is a question to Eve about God, as though God were not there.
Do you see what is happening here? The actual content of the
question is less important than the implied assumption behind
the question, implanted subconsciously through the exchange. It
is a seed of an idea: God is distant.[14] (So begins the dis-ease of
SSA.) If Eve takes the bait and responds to the question, she will
be entering into a conversation that serves to reinforce the power
of that idea in her own subconscious. She could have responded
to the serpent's question with something like, "Why don't you
ask God yourself? He is always near." Or called out to God,
"God, would you like to respond? This snake seems confused."[15]
Or Eve could have simply ignored the unwelcome talking snake.
But Satan makes the bait almost irresistible,[16] which leads to our
next point.

Third, the serpent seems confused. He is masquerading as the
fumbling detective Columbo of the animal kingdom. Remember,
one of the serpent's goals is to engage Eve in a conversation about
God as though God were not there. The question plants that seed,
and if Eve responds, she will water it, reinforce it, and perhaps
come to believe it. And so the serpent asks a question that invites
an immediate response. In essence, the serpent says, "Did God
really put you in this garden filled with all kinds of food options
and then tell you that you can't eat anything? Did God make
you only to starve you to death? What kind of creepy weirdo
is this God?"[17] Of course, Eve is motivated to quickly correct
this slanderous misunderstanding of her Creator. And the correc-
tion to this confusion should be easy—the serpent's question is

low-hanging fruit (pun intended).[18] Eve, as we know, opens her mouth and takes the bait, hook, line, and sinker.

In this moment we see the origin of religion, or at the very least, the origin of the context that makes religion possible: *the evil idea that God is distant and disinterested, and the resulting idea that it's up to us to do something about it.* This idea of a distant, detached, and dispassionate deity also invites a question—*Why is God distant?*—which we rush to respond to because theology abhors a vacuum. In our spiritual insecurity, we hypothesize that God might be distant because God is not good, or does not care, or does not love us the way we ache to be loved. (Certainly, the serpent's questioning moves our minds in this direction.) Religion thrives when our minds can be manipulated to spiritually catastrophize.

And so what happens next is more overtly religious than many realize.

THE FIRST SEMINARY

Here we have Eve and the devil talking about God as though God were not there. God's word has become a topic for discussion and dissection apart from the need for real relationship. Theology apart from friendship. And that's the problem with dissecting any living thing—you have to kill it first.

THE FIRST SERMON

In responding to the serpent, Eve says: "We may eat fruit from the trees in the garden, but God did say, 'You must not eat fruit from the tree that is in the middle of the garden, and you must not touch it, or you will die'" (Genesis 3:2-3). Eve creates the first religious rule, the first "fence around the law" (see chapter 10 in *The End of Religion*) by adding "and you must not touch it," something God never actually said. Eve's sermon is mostly correct, but like most preachers, she talks too long and says too much.

THE FIRST SERVICE

We mustn't forget that Eve is not conversing with the serpent alone. Adam is there "with her" (verse 6), listening passively, without engaging. This is the emptiness of religion—participants going through the motions without their hearts really in it, all form without substance.

THE FIRST SACRAMENT

Eve gives the forbidden fruit to Adam and they partake together. *Dominus vobiscum, quia Dominus non est in nobis* ("The Lord be with you, for the Lord is not with us") now becomes their liturgy.

NAKED AND AFRAID

Before Adam and Eve sinned, they succumbed to the religious impulse to bridge a gap between God and us—a gap that was never there in the first place. Ironically, by choosing sin over God, we create actual alienation between God and us, and become enemies in our minds (see Colossians 1:21)—a relational chasm God himself closes through Christ.

If we believe the lie that God has gone away or turned his back on us, we will begin to experience spiritual separation anxiety at the subconscious level. God is our life. God is the air we breathe, the spiritual oxygen to our souls. We were made to live in God the way fish were made to swim in water. In God we live and move and have our being (Acts 17:28). When Eve engaged with the serpent in a conversation about God as though God were not there, she opened herself up to a kind of spiritual panic attack. She may have felt at some subconscious level that her life was being squeezed from her lungs, as some constricting serpents will do when they attack.

After their fear of God's distance and disinterest has done its work, Adam and Eve are the ones who try to keep their distance, motivated by a new fear: fear of judgment. It is fear of divine judgment, wrath, and condemnation that becomes the emotional rocket fuel for propelling all religious development, and one that will ultimately be undone only by an extreme infusion of pure, perfect love (1 John 4:18). Adam and Eve sew fig leaves together to cover their nakedness, and then they try to hide from God behind some trees (Genesis 3:7-10). Adam and Eve have changed. They have moved from naked and unashamed (Genesis 2:25) to naked and afraid. God has not changed. God will now prob-lem-solve on their behalf out of the same love that gave birth to humankind in the first place. We, however, have become compli-cated, complex, and religious in the worst sense of the word. The rituals we sew together to hide our spiritual shame are not only futile but completely unnecessary. And yet God meets us where we are. God doesn't rip off our religious fig leaves, but instead makes them unnecessary by providing something "better" (Gene-sis 3:21; Hebrews 7:19, 22; 8:6). But only when the time is right and we are ready (Galatians 4:4-5).

The relationally corrosive effects of sin and shame and fear are immediately seen in Adam and Eve. They become the first (but not the last) to play the blame-and-shame game, accusing each other, the serpent, and even God for their poor choices (Genesis 3:12-13). Now this story of humankind exposes our ongoing pat-tern: even though we deeply desire intimacy, humans habitually distance ourselves, not only from God, but also from one another.

There is a word for "sin" used in the Greek New Testament Scriptures that is helpful here: *hamartia*, "to miss the mark." The etymology of *hamartia* exposes the human predicament. *Hamartia* comes from two words: *ha*, a negating word meaning "not," and *meros*, meaning "to be a part of" or "together with." So *sin* means to *not* be a part of what we were meant to be together with (like an arrow not being together with the target, or headphones not being plugged into a music source). In other words, *sin is sep-aration from our significance. Sin* is a truth-telling word referring to that corrosive force that causes relational disintegration. *Sin is relational rot.* It separates people, divides groups, and fractures our own minds.

This horror story of the disruption, disintegration, and decay of relationship all begins with our susceptibility to spiritual sepa-ration anxiety. It is this lie of God's distance and disinterest, and our assumed responsibility to bridge the gap, that is the essence and origin of all religion. Eve's subconscious separation anxiety, implanted by the devil himself, may not be the first sin, but it created the context for the first sin, because when we are expe-riencing spiritual separation anxiety, we make unhealthy choices born out of existential angst and deep-seated dread. And so, one might say, *it was the religious mindset that became the primordial ooze out of which crawled the first sin and the fall of humankind.* But now, a note of hope: there is a cure.

Lisa Sharon Harper writes: "Sin is not about the personal imperfection of the self. Rather, sin is any act that breaks any of the relationships God declared very good in the beginning. As a result, the antidote to sin is not personal perfection—it is radical love!"[19]

THE ANTIDOTE

Just a few verses later in Genesis 3, God pronounces a curse upon the serpent and says:

> And I will put hostility between you and the woman
> and between your offspring and her offspring;
> he will strike your head,
> and you will strike his heel.
> (Genesis 3:15 NET)

God says that a descendent of Eve, a human, will deliver the fatal blow to the head of the serpent. But not without being wounded himself. Right away, when Adam and Eve first sinned, God was right by their side offering hope.[20]

The antidote to religion is not secularism but "faith working through love" (Galatians 5:6 LEB)—our simple trust in the original narrative of God's attentive love, compassionate care, and purposeful calling upon our lives to live in partnership with him. Jesus gives us the evidence to rest our faith upon, because in Jesus, God forever fuses his own self with human reality. Whatever gap we created, real or imagined, is closed by Christ. And now, through spiritual practice (like prayer, meditation, Scripture reading, etc.), we don't seek to achieve any spiritual status we are not already offered as a gift. Instead, all spiritual practice becomes *a ministry of reminding* that God's gifts of love and life and light are already ours.

When we pray, we push back against the master deception of a distant deity. When we meditate on the teaching of Jesus, we tune our hearts into the ultimate truth of God's intimate presence. And when we worship through music and liturgy, we are reminding ourselves that God is for us, not against us.

Ultimately, spiritual practice is an opportunity to remind ourselves of what Jesus has already manifested into this world— Emmanuel, God with us (Matthew 1:23).

GOD'S RORSCHACH TEST

"Wait a minute," I've heard some religious people object. "God wasn't just offering hope. Don't make him out to be too nice! God isn't a namby-pamby grandpa in the sky. God burns with holy wrath. He cursed Adam and Eve, killed an animal to show them the high cost of sin, and then kicked them out of the garden!"

When a theology that prefers to see God primarily as the angry Father and the punishing Sovereign influences our reading of Scripture, the Bible becomes a sort of inkblot test that tells us more about our own psyche than it does about God.[21] If you read through Genesis 3, you'll see that God never curses his image bearers, though he does curse the serpent and the ground. And the only reason the text gives for God apparently killing an animal and then removing Adam and Eve from the garden is protection and provision, not punishment:

> The LORD God made garments of skin for Adam and his wife and clothed them. And the LORD God said, "The man has now become like one of us, knowing good and evil. He must not be allowed to reach out his hand and take also from the tree of life and eat, and live forever." So the LORD God banished him from the Garden of Eden to work the ground from which he had been taken. (Genesis 3:21-23)

This is God showing care and compassion, not consternation and condemnation. First God makes more durable clothing for Adam and Eve than their flimsy fig leaf aprons. Then God prevents them from eating from the tree of life and living forever in their now-fallen state. (The same kind of extreme compassion can be observed in the next chapter of the Bible when God protects Cain after he murders his brother Abel.)

Adam and Eve and their offspring now need a new way forward—one that will include death and resurrection, the end of the old and the beginning of something completely new. Through Jesus, God himself will show us the way.

Appendix A

TOWARD A JESUS-CENTERED SPIRITUAL PRACTICE

It's not about religion, it's about relationship." In *The End of Religion* I have argued that inside this cute cliché lies some buried treasure. Still, what does a "relationship" with Jesus look like? A fulsome answer to this question will need to be the topic of another book (and I recommend some good ones in appendix B). But for now, let me share some simple first steps toward moving from merely *believing* that you are loved by God and a friend of Jesus (John 15:15) to *behaving* like it too.

The great freedom and frustration of following Jesus is that the forms our faith takes—that is, the ways we relate to God—are as diverse as we are. There are some foundational basics—like prayer, Scripture study, gathering together for worship, and moving into the world with compassion—but the *way* we pray, learn, worship, and love others well can be very diverse.

I once heard a woman who had converted from nominal Christianity to Islam say, "As a Muslim, I am told exactly how to pray and exactly when to pray, and that is how I pray. When I was a Christian, I knew I could pray any time of day in any way I wanted. And for me that meant I never prayed." I get that. Many of us are incapacitated by wide-open freedom of choice. We thrive with specific directions and clear guidelines. The good news is, Jesus offers us some guidance for prayer, and other followers of Jesus have shared their experiences and approaches ever since.

What follows is a skeletal outline of three simple spiritual practices that have helped me draw closer to God as my Father and Jesus as my friend: (1) praying the Lord's Prayer, (2) Still Hear meditation, and (3) practicing the presence.

ONE: PRAYING THE "OUR FATHER" (THE LORD'S PRAYER)

Jesus gave some basic guidelines to his disciples about how to pray:

> And when you pray, do not be like the hypocrites, for they love to pray standing in the synagogues and on the street corners to be seen by others. Truly I tell you, they have received their reward in full. But when you pray, go into your room, close the door and pray to your Father, who is unseen. Then your Father, who sees what is done in secret, will reward you. And when you pray, do not keep on babbling like pagans, for they think they will be heard because of their many words. Do not be like them, for your Father knows what you need before you ask him.

> This, then, is how you should pray:

> "Our Father in heaven,
> hallowed be your name,
> your kingdom come,
> your will be done,
>   on earth as it is in heaven.
> Give us today our daily bread.
> And forgive us our debts,
>   as we also have forgiven our debtors.
> And lead us not into temptation,
>   but deliver us from the evil one."
> (Matthew 6:5-13)

Pray privately. Prayer, says Jesus, should not become an opportunity to piously parade our faith in front of others. Instead, we should make time to be by ourselves to practice reminding ourselves how truly *not* by ourselves we actually and always are. (This does not negate corporate prayer with others, which the early church practiced, but does put the emphasis on personal, private prayer.)

Prayer is not meant to be performative, but formative. Prayer is rooted in the conviction that we are already loved by a God who wants to spend time with us, not to hear our shopping list (God already knows what we need), but because talking together about what matters most is the stuff of friendship. And when we allow that conviction to lead us to pray, praying itself reinforces our faith in that conviction.

Pray daily. Notice that Jesus says we should pray for the bread we need for "today." This reminds us that everything good that comes into our lives every day is ultimately (directly or indirectly through others) a gift from God. But when will I pray about tomorrow? The answer is, tomorrow. Then it will be "today." Jesus says, "Therefore do not worry about tomorrow, for tomorrow will worry about itself. Each day has enough trouble of its own" (Matthew 6:34).

For instance, let's say that this Friday you have a major exam at school (or a significant presentation at work, or an important dental appointment) that you are anxious about. Rather than pray every day of the week, "Dear God, help me pass that exam on Friday," instead every day you pray, "Dear God, help me study well today and to feel peace about my preparation." When will you pray about Friday? On Friday! Every day, says Jesus, be fully present to that day's needs, struggles, and joys.

Pray out loud. Why does Jesus recommend *getting alone* to pray? Can't we pray while walking down the street or riding on the bus? Yes, we sure can. We can pray any way at any time in any place, and we should (1 Thessalonians 5:17). But between those wide-open times of praying whenever, wherever, however we want, we should have a daily time to focus and pray *out loud.* That's right—out loud. The idea of silently praying a thought-prayer in your head was not part of ancient Jewish culture. For Jesus, prayer is primarily something that involves the mind *and* the mouth, our brains *and* our bodies.

If you're not used to praying out loud, at first it can seem strange and stressful. But very soon you will realize that the most stressful part of prayer was praying silently in your mind and trying to stay focused. Praying out loud helps our mind focus by forming thoughts into words, and then reinforces those thoughts by hearing our own words as they enter back into our ears. Your "out loud" may be a booming voice or a quiet whisper, but don't miss this opportunity to involve your mind and your mouth together.

Pray conversationally. Now, we all know it takes less than thirty seconds to recite the Lord's Prayer. Yet we know that Jesus and his first followers prayed for much longer periods of time (e.g., Matthew 26:40-41). That's why I think Jesus meant for the Lord's Prayer to be a topical guideline, not a verbatim script.

So let's get specific. Here is an example of how I use the Lord's Prayer as a framework for a time of daily reflection and communion with God. I quote a line from the prayer (usually from the King James Version, since I have that one memorized from childhood), and then I let those words lead me into thematic conversation with God, praying out loud and taking time to quietly listen. It goes something like this:

Our Father which art in heaven, Hallowed be thy name.

"Thank you, Father, that you are *our* Father and not just *my* Father. I thank you that right now I am supernaturally connected by your Spirit with your children everywhere in the world, some who are also praying at this moment."

(I may sit with this reality for a minute and let it soak in.)

"And, Father, I want to tell you how much I love you, for you are holy, unlike anything or anyone else, complete love. I am so grateful to be your child and to be in your presence right here and right now."

> (I might take a while to declare to God other things about him that I believe to be true. This is called "praise," and it is the romance of our heavenly relationship.)

Thy kingdom come, Thy will be done in earth, as it is in heaven.

"I ask that your will and your way would hold sway in this world today, starting with me. Please show me any area of my life that is not moving in the flow of your loving ways. And give me the direction I need for today to partner with you in experiencing and extending the kingdom of heaven on earth."

> (And I may pause and just listen.)

Give us this day our daily bread.

> (This is the time I think about my own needs and the needs of others around me. I try not to fill up my time focusing on my *wants*, and instead try to focus on what I believe is worth praying about because it is a *need* for me or for others I know to be equipped to experience and extend the kingdom of heaven on earth. Sometimes God reminds me that I really have all the "bread" I need for today, and that he wants to use me to bring needed "bread" into the lives of others. What a privilege to partner with God to help answer the prayers of other people!)

And forgive us our debts, as we forgive our debtors.

"Father, please show me ways I might have hurt or sinned against others around me since last I prayed, yesterday."

> (And then I wait and let God help me see ways I can do better in my relationships. As examples come to mind, I thank God for his forgiveness, and I let go of any possible shame attached to my failure. At the same time, I may jot down the name of

someone whom God is gently nudging me to follow up with, to apologize to, to get right with, and to make sure nothing painful or destructive is building up between us.)

"And now, Father, please show me anyone who has hurt me or sinned against me in some way, on purpose or unknowingly, whom I might be tempted to hold something against. Help me see any ways, small or large, that I am sitting in judgment over someone."

(And then I wait and let God show me even tiny infractions against me or disappointments that have hurt me, and I breathe forgiveness in response and let it go. This is such a beautiful, restorative, life-giving practice to participate in daily, before relational resentments get the chance to grow.)

And lead us not into temptation, but deliver us from evil.

"Father, please show me those areas in my life where I am making excuses for my sin and selfishness, or where I might be walking toward temptation, and give me the courage to walk away. Please lead me, Lord, in this moment, in the right direction."

(Then I wait and let God show me those potential places, people, or activities that I may need to avoid or be more alert to regarding their potential negative effect. If I can't avoid them, I will ask God to help me bring light into those places, people, and activities to help me be the positive influence God has made me to be.)

For thine is the kingdom, and the power, and the glory, for ever.

"Father, I choose to focus on what is most important. Please raise my gaze from my own trivia, disappointments, and fears to find my delight in your eternal kingdom, power, and glory."

(And I close by quietly meditating on and resting in God's glorious agape love.)

Amen.

TWO: STILL HEAR MEDITATION

Sometimes I use the Lord's Prayer to guide my conversation with God. Other times, I use a passage of the Bible I am currently studying or learning from to become the basis for a time of talking with God and quiet meditation.

One day when my friend Don asked me to spend a few hours praying together, I thought that was a long time to fill the silence with our prayers. When we began to pray, I bowed my head and closed my eyes, wondering what my first words might be, and I heard Don open his Bible and start turning pages, letting *God* speak the first words by reading a passage of Scripture. I learned that day about open Bible praying.

Don turned prayer into a conversation with God by letting God start the interaction and set the theme. This is so meaningful, since much of the time people's prayers can become all about themselves. Over the years, I've come to combine Bible reading, prayer, and meditation into one spiritual practice I call "Still Hear" meditation.

Here is a general outline of how I structure my times of Still Hearing:

Preparation

1. Find a Bible that is easy for you to read. The NIV (New International Version), NLT (New Living Translation), and CEB (Common English Bible) are some of many easy-to-read translations available today. I recommend using a physical paper Bible rather than an onscreen version—our phone and computer screens are places of ongoing distraction and stress, and they represent a world I want to step away from for a few minutes to be still, to be present, and to hear the voice of Jesus. Sometimes having two or three translations available (yes, I have a Bible collection) can be helpful. If something isn't making sense in a passage of Scripture, sometimes reading the same passage in a different translation brings the clarity you're looking for.

2. Get a journal for note-taking and a pen or pencil for mark-
   ing up your Bible. (Don't be afraid to underline, circle words,
   and write in the margins of your Bible.) During your time of
   "Still Hearing," if you remember something you need to get
   done or think about something you want to come back to
   later, simply write these things down so you can let them go
   for now and are no longer distracted. They will be waiting
   for you when you are finished.

3. Find a place where you can be most at peace and least distracted. Jesus calls this our "inner room" (Matthew 6:6),
   and he often withdrew to quiet places to pray (Luke 5:16).

4. It might be a good idea to set a timer so you don't have
   to be checking your watch as you go. Five minutes is fine.
   Ten minutes is good. Twenty is better. Eventually, spending
   close to an hour a few days of the week in focused stillness
   and listening through reading, prayer, and meditation can
   become a welcome norm for many of us.

5. Choose a passage of the Bible that you want to sit with and
   learn from. I recommend starting with (and returning often
   to) the teachings of Jesus, like the Sermon on the Mount
   (found in Matthew 5–7 or see Luke 6) or a collection of
   his parables (as in Matthew 13 or Luke 15). You can work
   your way through the Gospels (the gospel of John is classic),
   then branch out into other parts of the New Testament (I
   especially like Romans, Galatians, Ephesians, Philippians,
   Colossians, James, 1 Peter, and 1 John), and then move back
   into Psalms in the Old Testament or the book of Genesis.

Practice

6. WELCOME the presence of Jesus and invite him to be your
   teacher. (Jesus is always with us, but this is our chance to
   tune in and become consciously awake to and aware of
   his reality.)

7. READ a Bible passage. It may be a full chapter or might be
   just a few verses. In the Gospels, I recommend one topical
   section, which is usually less than an entire chapter. Most

Bible publishers provide subheadings for these different sections (these topical chunks of text are called *pericopes*). Read the pericope slowly, in different translations if possible, and process it thoughtfully. (One of the things we often forget to make time for is simply *thinking*.) Engage your imagination, putting yourself in the scene, listening to and observing Jesus and others around him. What do you see and hear and smell and sense around you? While walking through the passage, if you have unanswered questions about something you don't understand, jot them down in your journal and make a point to ask a friend about them later, then move on. You don't have to understand everything in a reading in order for God to say something important to you through that passage.[1]

8. PRAY through the passage. Now that you've read through the chapter or pericope and feel familiar with it, start again at the beginning and pray your way through the passage. Read a verse (out loud), and pause to listen. Then talk to God (out loud) about the ideas in this verse as they connect with your own life. Then pause again and listen. Then move on to the next verse, and so on. Read. Listen. Pray. Listen. Repeat. This practice combines Bible reading and prayer together into something that turns both into a living conversation.

9. MEDITATE on whatever thought, verse, phrase, or word that Jesus seems to have highlighted for you during your time of study and prayer. Usually there will be one or two things in the passage that have stood out to you while reading through the text imaginatively. Sometimes the Holy Spirit seems to use a highlighter to point out a word or phrase we need to pay attention to. This will be our focus for meditation.[2] Take some slow, deep breaths, inviting the Spirit of Christ to fill your consciousness. The word for "spirit" and "breath" is the same word in the Bible (*ruach* in Hebrew and *pneuma* in Greek), so intentional, deep breathing can be an appropriate invitational prayer with our body for the infilling of God's Spirit. Relax and fill your mind with this highlighted thought from the passage—always connecting

that thought to the highest reality: *God is love.* Be aware that the same Spirit who inspired the text you just read is now in you and around you helping move your mind toward love and light and life. Let yourself move with rather than against the flow of the Holy Spirit. Rest in that love as you simply focus on one simple thought, phrase, or word from the text. You may sit mentally still and silent with that one word pictured in your mind, or you may repeat the word or phrase quietly yet out loud over and over again. Try to stay with this practice for a few minutes (two to five minutes is a great beginner goal). As you do this, God may help move from your head down to your heart the reality that the word or phrase points to. If Bible reading and prayer is like typing truth into our lives, meditation is like hitting the Enter key.

10. MOVE on with your day. When your Still Hear time is done, see how long you can keep conscious of the presence of Jesus. In one sense, the most important part of any time of Bible study happens when we close the Bible. The most important part of prayer or meditation happens when we stop and stand and walk out our door. These are the moments when we see whether we are committed to apply what we've learned and give what we've been given. It's also our opportunity to carry the consciousness of Christ with us throughout our day as we "rejoice always, pray without ceasing, give thanks in all circumstances; for this is the will of God in Christ Jesus for you" (1 Thessalonians 5:16-18 NRSV).

This practice of spending time daily recalibrating our focus and softening our hearts in the manifest presence of Jesus will help us unhitch our hearts from the pull of religious judgmentalism on the one side and the pull of our own fear-based, anxiety-saturated, self-preserving impulses on the other. During these "Still Hear" times, some of us may have emotional experiences of God's unconditional, accepting love. Others of us may experience a deep conviction of our conscience over something hurtful we have done or failed to do, and the reassurance of God's forgiveness and guidance to make it right. Sometimes we may sense the actual presence of Christ with us, reminding us of his compassion and care. And many of us will simply have times of quiet calm that allow us to move with the flow of the Spirit to produce more of the fruit of love in our lives (Galatians 5:22-23). Remember, we are not trying to manufacture a particular experience; we are simply waking up to and experiencing what has been true all along.[3]

In *The God-Shaped Brain*, psychiatrist Timothy Jennings says:

> Brain research shows that fifteen minutes a day in meditation or thoughtful communion with the God of love results in measurable development of the prefrontal cortex, especially in the anterior cingulate cortex (ACC). This is the area where we experience love, compassion and empathy. The healthier the ACC, the calmer the amygdala (alarm center), and the less fear and anxiety we experience. Truly, love casts out all fear![4]

When our minds are focused on and filled with love, there is no room for fear (1 John 4:18). To quote Jennings again:

> Imagine stepping out into the street and, as you do, you see an eighteen-wheeler bearing down on you. What emotion do you experience? Fear! Imagine your three-year-old son toddles out into that same street. Now the eighteen-wheeler is bearing down on him. There is just enough time to run and push your child out of the way, but if you do, you will get hit. What do you do? You push your child out of the way! And as you see your child roll to safety in the grass, what emotion do you experience? Joy! In both situations you are being hit by a truck; in the first, there is only fear, but in the second, love has vanquished fear.[5]

THREE: PRESENCE PRACTICE

As we spend more daily time practicing Still Hear meditation, we will become increasingly aware of the voice of Jesus speaking to us through Scripture, in our hearts, and in our world. Listening to Jesus in stillness will help us get better over time at hearing and recognizing his voice while we walk through all the activities of our daily lives. Granted, when Jesus speaks to us through nature, art, circumstances, and other people, his voice may not always be as clear as it is through his own recorded teachings in Scripture. This is also true when Jesus speaks to and through his Spirit directly into our heart while we are engaged in the many activities of our day rather than when we are still, quiet, and attentive. We may wonder, "Is that the guidance of Christ in me? Or is that just me telling myself something that I want to hear?" But over time, we will be able to tune in to the voice of Jesus wherever we go and whatever we're doing. Getting to know his voice *in Scripture first* is the key to recognizing his voice everywhere else.

For centuries, Christ-followers have engaged in a spiritual activity designed to help us tune in to the voice and presence of Jesus at all times, not just in stillness and quietness. This spiritual discipline is known by many names, but probably the most common is "practicing the presence of God," popularized by the writings of a Carmelite monk named Brother Lawrence of the Resurrection (1614–91). I've recommended some good books in appendix B that could help you develop this practice, but for now, here is how I have approached presence practice.

After spending my daily quiet time in Still Hear meditation, I make it my goal to keep the awareness of the guiding presence of Jesus in my consciousness for as long as I can. This might last a minute, or five minutes, or longer. Eventually my mind will be swept up with the activities of the day, and when I notice I have been ignoring the presence of Jesus, I simply say a mental hello again, or simply smile at the joy of being reminded I am not alone, and I continue my awareness as I move forward with my day. Sometimes I use tools to help remind me of the presence of Christ. I will put visual reminders, like sticky notes on which I've simply written "Jesus," in places where I will see them throughout my day—my bathroom mirror, my computer screen, my office desk, the dashboard of my car, and my refrigerator (now let's move on because that's way too convicting). I've also tried setting my phone alarm to go off at different intervals throughout my day to remind me that Jesus is with me.

I remember one time playing with one of my daughters when she was little, tossing her up in the air and enjoying her laughter, when my reminding alarm went off. It hit me then that Jesus was with us, enjoying her laughter, too, and the entire experience became spiritually enriched and infused with supernatural joy. I still remember that moment now years later, and it continues to make me smile in my soul, thanks to this one spiritual practice. Over time, what at first takes effort will become natural and normal. Your conscious mind will become more alert, awake, and at home in the presence of the friendliness, kindness, and consciousness of Christ. Every so often you may return to using visual or audible reminders of God's presence for a season of time, to exercise your mental powers of spiritual perception. Now you will be doing life together with the one who loves you most, awake and alert to just how marvelous and penetrated with love your life really is.

Once you feel more attuned to practicing the presence of God, you may want to incorporate "practicing the presence of people." In this exercise, we make it our mental goal to hold one primary thought front and center about each person we interact with throughout our day: *I am in the presence of someone who is infinitely precious to God, an image of the Almighty, and I am so grateful for this honor.* As you interact with and honor them accordingly, the world around you and inside you will change. You will become less judgmental and more loving, more filled with gratitude and joy.

We all have tapes of judgment about people playing in our minds. We ask judgmental questions continually (why would anyone wear *that?* or listen to *that?* or act like *that?*), and we put people into categories of judgment (balding man / short woman / old fart / cocky teenager / annoying kid / loud talker, and so on). These thoughts are so prevalent, we barely notice that *we are judgment machines.* Eventually, our minds wrap up the people we know in our own judgmental labels (Pontificating Pete; Too Much Makeup Mary; Awkward Andrew; Boring Bob; Super Smart Sue; Sexy Sam). Some of these labels that we subconsciously wrap people in can seem like compliments, but when we distill anyone down to any one primary characteristic other than that person's infinite worth and value as an image bearer of God, we diminish that person's humanity.

The apostle Paul said: "Do nothing out of selfish ambition or vain conceit. Rather, in humility *value others above yourselves,* not looking to your own interests but each of you to the interests of the others" (Philippians 2:3-4; emphasis mine). To value others above ourselves does not mean we diminish our value in the least. It does mean, among other things, that we enter into our daily interactions with others in *a posture of learning.* We will want to pay attention to people, believing there is nothing more precious on this planet than the human being who is right in front of us at this moment.

Practicing the presence of people can make space for the love of Jesus to flow through us toward others, which in turn will help us encounter Jesus in those relationships. We will become more loving, and we will encounter more love in every interaction of our lives. Remember: Every person you will meet today is an infinitely precious image bearer of God, and you are honored to be in each person's presence.

Appendix B

CONTINUING EDUCATION

Time to recommend some books, podcasts, and other online opportunities for digging deeper.

On the gospel, the irreligious good news of Jesus . . .
- Matthew W. Bates, *Gospel Allegiance*
- Gregory A. Boyd, *Repenting of Religion*
- Bruxy Cavey, *Reunion: The Good News of Jesus for Seekers, Saints, and Sinners*
- Bruxy Cavey, *Reunion: A Study Guide*
- Andrew Farley, *Relaxing with God*
- Andrew Farley, *The Perfect You*
- Lisa Sharon Harper, *The Very Good Gospel*
- Brad Jersak, *A More Christlike God*
- Scot McKnight, *The King Jesus Gospel*
- Brian D. McLaren, *The Secret Message of Jesus*
- John Ortberg, *Eternity Is Now in Session*
- N. T. Wright, *Simply Good News*
- Brian Zahnd, *Sinners in the Hands of a Loving God*

On Jesus in his first-century context . . .
- Kenneth E. Bailey, *Jesus through Middle Eastern Eyes*
- Donald Kraybill, *The Upside-Down Kingdom*
- N. T. Wright, *The Challenge of Jesus*

- N. T. Wright and Michael F. Bird, *The New Testament in Its World*

On the atoning death of Jesus . . .
- Mark Baker, *Recovering the Scandal of the Cross*
- Darrin W. Snyder Belousek, *Atonement, Justice, and Peace*
- Keith Giles, *Jesus Unforsaken*
- Michael J. Gorman, *The Death of the Messiah and the Birth of the New Covenant*
- Fleming Rutledge, *The Crucifixion*
- N. T. Wright, *The Day the Revolution Began*

On Anabaptist spirituality . . .
- Palmer Becker, *Anabaptist Essentials*
- Harold S. Bender, *The Anabaptist Vision*
- Douglas Jacobsen and Rodney J. Sawatsky, *Gracious Christianity*
- Stuart Murray, *The Naked Anabaptist*
- Alfred Neufeld, *What We Believe Together*
- C. Arnold Snyder, *Following in the Footsteps of Christ*

On living the nonviolent, enemy-loving, peace-promoting, agape ethic of Jesus . . .
- Sharon L. Baker Putt, *A Nonviolent Theology of Love*
- Gregory A. Boyd, *The Myth of a Christian Nation*
- Shane Claiborne and Chris Haw, *Jesus for President*
- Matthew Curtis Fleischer, *Jesus the Pacifist*
- Charles E. Moore, *Peace Matters*
- Ronald J. Sider, *If Jesus Is Lord*
- Ronald J. Sider, *Speak Your Peace*
- Preston Sprinkle, *Fight*
- Brian Zahnd, *A Farewell to Mars*

On becoming a growing, maturing Jesus-follower . . .
- Timothy R. Jennings, *The God-Shaped Brain*
- Timothy R. Jennings, *The God-Shaped Heart*
- Brad Jersak, *A More Christlike Way*

- Mark Scandrette, *Practicing the Way of Jesus*
- James Bryan Smith, *The Good and Beautiful God / Life / Community* (series)
- Rich Villodas, *The Deeply Formed Life*
- Derek Vreeland, *By the Way*
- Dallas Willard, *The Divine Conspiracy*
- Norman Wirzba, *Way of Love*

On spiritual practices . . .
- Gregory A. Boyd, *Present Perfect*
- Gregory A. Boyd, *Seeing Is Believing*
- Richard J. Foster, *Celebration of Discipline*
- Natalie Frisk, *Raising Disciples*
- Brad Jersak, *Can You Hear Me?*
- Brother Lawrence, *The Practice of the Presence of God*
- Mike Mason, *Practicing the Presence of People*
- Scot McKnight, *The Blue Parakeet*
- Ken Shigematsu, *Survival Guide for the Soul*
- Charles Stanley, *The Spirit-Filled Life*
- Danielle Strickland, InfinitumLife.com
- Rich Villodas, *The Deeply Formed Life*
- Dallas Willard, *The Spirit of the Disciplines*
- Dallas Willard, *Hearing God*

On faith and doubt . . .
- Andy Bannister, *The Atheist Who Didn't Exist*
- Gregory A. Boyd, *Benefit of the Doubt*
- Gregory A. Boyd, *Letters from a Skeptic*
- Justin Brierley, *Unbelievable?*
- Timothy Keller, *Making Sense of God*
- Timothy Keller, *The Reason for God*

On issues of social justice and Christian compassion . . .
- Beth Allison Barr, *The Making of Biblical Womanhood*
- Mae Elise Cannon and Andrea Smith, *Evangelical Theologies of Liberation and Justice*
- James Cone, *The Cross and the Lynching Tree*

- Kaitlin B. Curtice, *Native*
- Lisa Sharon Harper, *The Very Good Gospel*
- Drew Hart, *Trouble I've Seen*
- Drew Hart, *Who Will Be a Witness?*
- Willie James Jennings, *The Christian Imagination: Theology and the Origin of Race*
- Osheta Moore, *Dear White Peacemakers*
- John Perkins, *Dream with Me*
- Don Posterski, *Jesus on Justice*
- Danielle Strickland, *Better Together*
- Richard Twiss, *Rescuing the Gospel from the Cowboys*
- Mirslav Volf, *Exclusion and Embrace*
- Cynthia Long Westfall, *Paul and Gender*
- Dan White Jr., *Love over Fear*

On understanding the Bible, Christian theology, and Jesus-centricity . . .
- Bruxy Cavey, *Jesus 101*
- Tim Day, *God Enters Stage Left*
- John Dickson, *A Doubter's Guide to the Bible*
- Keith Giles, *Jesus Unbound*
- Meghan Larissa Good, *The Bible Unwrapped*
- Brad Jersak, *A More Christlike Word*
- Glen Scrivener, *Long Story Short*
- Andy Stanley, *Irresistible*
- Don Thorson, *An Exploration of Christian Theology*
- *The Jesus Way: Small Books of Radical Faith*, a book series published by Herald Press
- *The Bible Project* (podcast and videos)—check out BibleProject.com
- *Jesus Collective* (a global community of Jesus-centered visionaries)—check out JesusCollective.com
- *The Meeting House (a church for people who aren't into church)*—check out teaching videos at TheMeetingHouse .com and join the discussion via a Home Church (online or in person)
- *Bruxy.com* is my website and blog on all things Jesus-y

NOTES

INTRODUCTION: ARE YOU READY TO RETHINK?

1 James Allan Francis, "One Solitary Life," in *The Real Jesus and Other Sermons* (Philadelphia: Judson Press, 1926).

2 I am paraphrasing an idea I learned from Jaroslav Pelikan, who was a professor of history at Yale University.

SESSION 6: TEMPLE, SYMBOLS, AND SACRIFICE

1 John Stott, *Why I Am a Christian* (Downers Grove, IL: Intervarsity, 2003), 62–63. Also see his wonderful work *The Cross of Christ* (Downers Grove, IL: Intervarsity, 2006), 335. First published 1986.

BONUS CHAPTER 1: THE FAITH INSTINCT

1 E. O. Wilson, *On Human Nature* (Cambridge, MA: Harvard University Press, 2004), 169.

2 Some date the beginning of the Neolithic period to about 8,000 BC rather than 10,000 BC, which would make this temple part of the late Mesolithic period. But who's counting.

3 Karen Armstrong, *A Short History of Myth* (Edinburgh: Canongate, 2005), 1. Also see Andrew Newberg, *Neurotheology: How Science Can Enlighten Us about Spirituality* (New York: Columbia University Press, 2018), 107.

4 This is confirmed by multiple scientific articles. In other apparent burial sites, the corpses seem to be placed in a sleeping position with a rock for a pillow. Did Neanderthals believe we sleep when we die, ready to wake up on the other side? Or did they believe that death is a form of rebirth? We don't know, but we do know that they believed something.

5 A phrase first coined by the famous sociologist and historian of religion Mircea Eliade.

6 Dean Hamer, *The God Gene: How Faith Is Hardwired into Our Genes* (New York: Anchor, 2005), 6, 82. Emphasis in the original.

7 John Stott, *Why I Am a Christian* (Downers Grove, IL: Intervarsity, 2003), 72, 98.

 8 Scot McKnight, *The King Jesus Gospel: The Original Good News Revisited* (Grand Rapids: Zondervan, 2011), 126.

 9 C. S. Lewis, *The Weight of Glory* (San Francisco: HarperSanFrancisco, 2001), 397. First published 1941. For a deeply insightful book on this issue, see *The Evidential Power of Beauty* by Thomas Dubay.

10 As far as I can find, the actual quote is "The young man who rings the bell at the brothel is unconsciously looking for God" and comes from a 1945 novel by Bruce Marshall called *The World, the Flesh, and Father Smith.*

11 Huston Smith, *The Soul of Christianity: Restoring the Great Tradition* (San Francisco: HarperSanFrancisco, 2005).

12 *The Matrix*, directed by Lana Wachowski and Lilly Wachowski (Hollywood, CA: Warner Bros., 1999).

13 Erich Fromm, *Psychoanalysis and Religion* (New Haven, CT: Yale University Press, 1950), 24.

14 Justin Barrett, *Why Would Anyone Believe in God?* (Lanham, MD: Altamira, 2004).

15 For more information about the biological basis of the human God-impulse, see Hamer, *The God Gene*; Andrew Newberg, Eugene d'Aquili, and Vince Rause, *Why God Won't Go Away: Brain Science and the Biology of Belief* (New York: Ballantine, 2002); Robert Buckman, *Can We Be Good without God? Biology, Behavior, and the Need to Believe* (Amherst, NY: Prometheus, 2002); and Newberg, *Neurotheology*. Books like these raise the question, Do we believe in God because we have evolved a brain wiring that causes faith, or because God has created us for faith? Either way, the books are conclusive: humans are hardwired for faith.

16 No doubt, the beauty and artistry of creation is infused with copious amounts of suffering, death, and horrendous evil. For many of us, this is the biggest stumbling block to faith in a good God. The cognitive dissonance is sometimes deafening and sometimes quiet as a whisper, but in a world of so much suffering, the problem of evil is always present. At the same time, we are stuck, because the very category of "evil" suggests that there is something like objective "good" infused into this universe. Otherwise, all the violence, pain, and suffering in our world, especially the horrors humans perpetrate upon one another, cannot be condemned with anything more than a shoulder shrug and a muttering of "Oh well, that's life." But we know intuitively that this is not the response horrendous evil deserves. Which brings us back full circle to the ethical-impulse, discussed later in this chapter.

17 Buckman, *Good without God?*, 188.

18 Mark Tabb, *Living with Less: The Upside of Downsizing Your Life* (Nashville: B&H Books, 2006), 9.

19 Personally, while I accept the idea of basic human *rights*, I am motivated more by the idea of universal human *responsibilities*. I believe I am made in the image and likeness of the Creator, and because of that, I am less inclined to think about my rights and more inclined to think about how I have been called into being to love others and care for creation.

20 Even societies that have practiced human sacrifice or cannibalism did so not as an act of devaluing human life but rather as the use of that

human value in an act of sacrifice to the gods, or as an act of aggression toward and intimidation of enemies. For instance, tribes in Papua New Guinea (where my wife lived and worked for a year) who engaged in cannibalism did so not because they put humans in the same category as pigs and chickens. For them, cannibalism was always a strategic means to intimidate and overpower the enemy. Cannibalism was never a category misunderstanding, but the ultimate act of psychological warfare. The threat of the horror of cannibalism actually helped keep peace between tribes. It was their version of the atom bomb and cold war. (On the shared dehumanizing violence of war and religion, recall chapter 26 from *The End of Religion.*)

21 This subgroup makes up about 10–13 percent of the population. See Megan Hull, ed., "Personality Disorders Facts and Statistics," The Recovery Village, last modified April 21, 2021, https://www. therecoveryvillage.com/mental-health/personality-disorders/related/ personality-disorder-statistics/.

22 The story of Christian apologist David Wood stands out to me in this regard (see "Misguided Man Assaults Father with Hammer," CBN, January 28, 2015, https://www1.cbn.com/video/misguided-man-assaults-father-with-hammer). Also see the story of the psychiatry professor James Fallon, who describes himself as a "pro-social psychopath" (see "How a Psychiatry Professor Accidentally Discovered He Was a Psychopath," CBC, last modified February 20, 2020, https://www.cbc.ca/radio/outintheopen/ impostors-1.4695876/how-a-psychiatry-professor-accidentally-discovered-he-was-a-psychopath-1.4705718).

23 John Calvin, *Commentaries on the First Book of Moses Called Genesis,* trans. John King (Grand Rapids: Christian Classics Ethereal Library), 52, 53. First published 1554.

24 *Luther's Works,* vol. 1, *Lectures on Genesis, Chapters 1–5,* ed. Jaroslav Pelikan, trans. George V. Schick (Saint Louis: Concordia, 1958), 63–64. Emphasis mine.

25 Augustine, *Confessions* 1.1.

26 See Jay Lombard, *The Mind of God: Neuroscience, Faith, and a Search for the Soul* (New York: Harmony Books, 2017), 33.

27 C. S. Lewis, *Mere Christianity* (San Francisco: HarperSanFrancisco, 2001). First published 1952.

28 Lewis, *Weight of Glory.*

29 Quoted in Jeffrey Kluger, "Is God in Our Genes?," *Time* 164, no. 17 (October 24, 2005), http://content.time.com/time/subscriber/article/0,33009,995465,00.html.

BONUS CHAPTER 2: THE ORIGIN OF RELIGION

1 This quote is from Stephen Hawking's book *The Grand Design* (New York: Bantam, 2010), written in partnership with physicist Leonard Mlondinow. I'm grateful to Glen Scrivener for drawing my attention to it through his excellent book *Long Story Short: The Bible in 12 Phrases* (Fearn, UK: Christian Focus Publications, 2018).

2 Philosophers call the creation of matter out of nothing (rather than
   preexisting matter) *creatio ex nihilo*. Now we can add to this the idea of
   creatio ex amore.

3 Scrivener, *Long Story Short*, 25.

4 As the story goes, God's riotous creativity calls everything into being
   over the period of a few "days." It's worth noting that the Hebrew word
   for "day" (*yom*) is a flexible word. *Yom* can refer to a twenty-four-hour
   day, or to only the daylight hours of a day (as in "day" versus "night"),
   or to an expansive season of time—as we might say in English, "back in
   the day." This is how *yom* is used in the very next chapter of Genesis. In
   Genesis 2:4, the author reflects back on the first *week* of creation and
   comments, "This is the account of the heavens and the earth when they
   were created, in the day [*yom*] that the Lord God made earth and heaven"
   (NASB). It is easy to miss this since many English translations translate
   the sentence more loosely, not using the word *day* at all. So do the six
   days of creation in Genesis 1 refer to an actual work week, or to a massive
   expanse of time, say, millions or billions of years? After all, the sun and
   moon (which help give us our concept of a day being roughly twenty-four
   hours) are not even created by God until the fourth "day"!

   Some scholars point out that even more interesting than the length of
   time described in the first chapter of Genesis is the *order* of creation. The
   Bible says God caused life to begin in the sea, then God brought reptiles
   and birds into being, and eventually mammals, including and concluding
   with humans. Now that's a familiar pattern. Was the Bible teaching that
   God created life on Earth through the mechanism of evolution thousands
   of years before the concept would even be observed and understood by
   humans? Maybe the whole "evolution versus creation" debate that some
   religious people get into is misguided. Maybe the Bible was way ahead of
   us, claiming from the start that when it comes to creation versus evolution,
   it is both/and, not either/or. Or maybe trying to explain our evolutionary
   origins was never the purpose of the opening chapters of Genesis. Maybe
   the author had something more important to communicate through this
   book of beginnings.

5 Did Adam and Eve literally exist? Attempting to answer this question with
   any considered thoughtfulness is well beyond the scope of this chapter. The
   best I can do is summarize some perspectives and suggest some sources for
   further study. While all Christians agree that the *message* and *meaning* of
   Genesis is true and truly revolutionary, they hold differing views on how
   to understand its historicity. Here are three Christian views:

   a. Literal. Young earth, literal text, six-day creation. We've all heard
   this view. It motivated the infamous Scopes Monkey Trial of 1925 and
   inspired at least one fascinating family theme park.

   b. Partial. The story of Adam and Eve is historical but was never
   meant to be the whole story of humanity, since according to Genesis 4,
   there are apparently other people living outside the garden of Eden at
   that time whose story is not told. According to this view, Genesis 1 is the
   worldwide story of all humanity, made in God's image. Genesis 2 is the

story of how God began to reveal Godself in creation through two specific humans in a specific place.

    c. Parable. The first chapters of Genesis are divinely inspired, meaningful myth, and literal history doesn't begin to be recorded until the twelfth chapter of the Bible with the story of Abraham. (After all, we know from Jesus that God likes to teach truth through the language of parables!)

    For more on these different perspectives, see James K. Hoffmeier, Gordon J. Wenham, and Kenton L. Sparks, *Genesis: History, Fiction, or Neither? Three Views on the Bible's Earliest Chapters*, Counterpoints (Grand Rapids, MI: Zondervan, 2015); Denis O. Lamoureux et al., *Four Views on the Historical Adam*, Counterpoints (Grand Rapids, MI: Zondervan, 2013); Dennis R. Venema and Scot McKnight, *Adam and the Genome: Reading Scripture after Genetic Science* (Grand Rapids, MI: Brazos, 2017); John H. Walton, *The Lost World of Genesis One: Ancient Cosmology and the Origins Debate* (Downers Grove, IL: IVP Academic, 2009); John H. Walton, *The Lost World of Adam and Eve: Genesis 2–3 and the Human Origins Debate* (Downers Grove, IL: IVP Academic, 2015); Denis O. Lamoureux, *I Love Jesus and I Accept Evolution* (Eugene, OR: Wipf and Stock, 2009); Denis O. Lamoureux, *Evolution: Scripture and Nature Say Yes!* (Grand Rapids, MI: Zondervan, 2016); Denis O. Lamoureux, *The Bible and Ancient Science* (Tullahoma, TN: McGahan, 2020); and S. Joshua Swamidass, *The Genealogical Adam and Eve: The Surprising Science of Universal Ancestry* (Downers Grove, IL: IVP Academic, 2019).

6 Lois Tverberg, *Walking in the Dust of Rabbi Jesus: How the Jewish Words of Jesus Can Change Your Life* (Grand Rapids, MI: Zondervan, 2012), 186.

7 Lisa Sharon Harper, *The Very Good Gospel: How Everything Wrong Can Be Made Right* (New York: Waterbrook, 2016), 32–33. Italic in the original.

8 I was once interviewed for a television show by a host who was unable to hide the chip on his shoulder toward me as a perceived representative of religion. (Obviously he hadn't read the first edition of my book!) Toward the end of the interview, he hit his crescendo with a final note of challenge: "Bruxy, just look around you. Look at human history and human present. Look at the pain and suffering all over this planet. It's evil! Don't you just have to admit that God screwed up?" I could understand where he was coming from, but I felt that he was missing the point. I responded, "No, the Bible tells me that God left us in charge of the planet, and we screwed up. Let's not blame God for a responsibility that is thoroughly ours." Then I added, "Besides, what gives you the idea that suffering is 'evil'? If there is no God, good and evil are philosophical categories of convenience devoid of any objective reality and suffering is simply a neutral part of how nature functions." I was never invited back on that show.

9 Adam and Eve are archetypal names. They represent all humankind. Adam's name (Heb. *Adam*) is connected to *adamah* (shout-out to *Battlestar Galactica* fans), the Hebrew word for "dirt." To be human (*ha'adam*)

is to be literally an "earthling"—a mix of the dust and the divine. And Eve is a translation of *hawwah*, which means "living," for she is said to be "the mother of all the living" (Genesis 3:20).

10 This raises the question, What is the Bible saying is wrong with knowledge about good and evil? I suspect the answer is nothing. Proverbs is an entire book of the Bible dedicated to this discernment, and Jesus regularly helps his followers recognize the way of love and reject any other way of being in this world. God knows that the knowledge of good and evil would be unnecessary if there were no evil in the world. Beyond that, if and when knowledge about good and evil would become important for humankind to learn, God would be our teacher. So here God is teaching patience and trust, not perpetual ignorance and infantilism.

11 More context for the origin of the serpent can be found in the last book of the Bible, in Revelation 12. As an aside, I have no trouble believing Satan is real. If pure good is more than a concept, but rather a Person we call "God," then I can embrace the Bible's idea that pure evil is also more than a philosophical category or abstract energy, and also a person. I think our universe is far more personal, far more relational, in good and evil ways, than any of us realize.

12 Ziony Zevit, *What Really Happened in the Garden of Eden?* (New Haven, CT: Yale University Press, 2013), 164.

13 This seems to be why the apostle Paul would later use the deception of Eve as an illustration and warning that we, male and female, should *all* learn from in 1 Corinthians 11:3. All believers are meant to experience God's grace directly, for themselves, not only indirectly through the stories and structures of others. This also helps explain early Christian hesitancy to establish women leaders in the church, as in 1 Timothy 2:12-14. In the first century, women would have been more susceptible to the weakness of secondhand-only knowledge of God's will and ways, since they were less likely to be literate or trained in Scripture interpretation. Women could be more easily deceived, like Eve, not because of some weakness inherent in their sex but because of their lack of direct encounter with God's Word. Thankfully, this is no longer the case and the church can benefit from the male and female aspects of God's image in humankind leading the church in partnership together.

14 I'm reminded of the word illustration GODISNOWHERE. Depending on one's frame of reference, different people will interpret the same data points to conclude "God is nowhere" or "God is now here."

15 Eve may have been thrown off about God's closeness because she and Adam may have been *outside* the garden of Eden when they crossed paths with the serpent. The garden of Eden was always intended to be home base for Adam and Eve to move out from and return to, but never for them to stay within. Remember their original mandate was to "fill the earth and subdue it" (Genesis 1:28).

16 In the Hebrew, this sentence uttered by the serpent is barely even a question. It is a kind of partial sentence inviting completion. See Zevit, *What Really Happened?*, 166–167.

17 The serpent is actually planting two slanderous seeds: (1) God is
    distant; and (2) God is unloving. Religion thrives in this toxic emo-
    tional environment.

18 Was this fruit an apple, as is often depicted in art and in the Apple Inc.
    "take a bite out of the tree of knowledge" logo? We don't know. As Zevit
    writes, "The Western tradition that it was an apple tree arose because
    of the assonance between the Latin words for wrongdoing, *malum*, and
    apple, *malus*. The association of apples with the Tree of Knowing lacks
    any basis in the Hebrew text." *What Really Happened?*, 170.

19 Harper, *Very Good Gospel*, 50.

20 Scholars refer to the declaration of hope in Genesis 3:15 as the *protoevan-
    gelium*, Latin for "the first gospel" or "the first proclamation of the good
    news of Jesus."

21 I realize that portions of the Bible could be used to paint the picture of
    God as a wrathful, punitive Sovereign. But when we start with Jesus
    as God's ultimate self-disclosure and interpret all other scriptural data
    through him (see John 1:18; 12:45), we arrive at a different picture.
    For more on this, see Greg Boyd's *Crucifixion of the Warrior God*
    (Minneapolis: Fortress, 2017), as well as his smaller book *Cross Vision:
    How the Crucifixion of Jesus Makes Sense of Old Testament Violence*
    (Minneapolis: Fortress, 2017), and his more recent *Inspired Imperfection:
    How the Bible's Problems Enhance Its Divine Authority* (Minneapolis:
    Fortress, 2020).

APPENDIX A: TOWARD A JESUS-CENTERED SPIRITUAL PRACTICE

1 Augustine of Hippo (c. 354–430) wrote that "the passage being read
   should be studied with careful consideration until its interpretation can
   be connected with the realm of love." *De Doctrina Christiana* 3.54. This
   makes good sense to me, since the Bible at its best should lead us to Jesus,
   and Jesus shows us that God is love.

2 There are two categories of meditation: *Apophatic* (the way of negation)
   meditation is about emptying the mind or simply accepting what is,
   without a particular focus or specific content. *Kataphatic* (the way of
   affirmation) meditation is about filling the mind with pure truth and love,
   and often uses a focus—an icon, a mental image, or a text. Both forms can
   be helpful. Still Hearing is a form of kataphatic meditation.

3 Some skeptics argue that just because we sense a personal presence
   doesn't make that presence real. See, e.g., John C. Wathey's *The Illusion
   of God's Presence: The Biological Origins of Spiritual Longing* (Amherst,
   NY: Prometheus, 2016). I agree and would not recommend making any
   personal emotional experience the *basis* for your trust in Jesus. But as I
   explain in chapter 16 of *The End of Religion*, my route to faith in Jesus
   is based on the miraculous explanatory power of his teachings, not on a
   mystical experience of his presence. Now I am inclined to trust Jesus in the
   things I cannot test, since he has shown himself supernaturally insightful
   and always trustworthy in the things I can test, namely, the cumulative

evidence found in the multiple ways the solutions found in Jesus' teachings match perfectly with the needs of my life and this world.

4 Timothy R. Jennings, *The God-Shaped Brain: How Changing Your View of God Transforms Us* (Grand Rapids, MI: Baker Books, 2017), 133.

5 Jennings, 203.

THE AUTHOR

Bruxy Cavey is the teaching pastor of The Meeting House—a church for people who aren't into church. This multisite, house church–based Anabaptist community in the Greater Toronto area exists to create safe places for spiritually curious people to ask questions and develop thoughtful faith. Bruxy is also the author of his bestselling book on the gospel—*Reunion: The Good News of Jesus for Seekers, Saints, and Sinners*—and its study guide. Bruxy and his wife, Nina, live in Hamilton, Ontario. They have three daughters, as well as other honorary adopted family.

For more information, you can find Bruxy on most social media platforms, or visit Bruxy.com, TheMeetingHouse.com, and JesusCollective.com.